* pg 16 & 17 Neocons
Wolfowitz

IS IRAQ ANOTHER VIETNAM?

IS IRAQ
ANOTHER VIETNAM?

Robert K. Brigham

PublicAffairs · New York

Book design and composition by Mark McGarry, Texas Type & Book Works
Set in Dante

Library of Congress Cataloging-in-Publication Data is available
from the Library of Congress

ISBN-13: 978-1-58648-413-2
ISBN-10: 1-58648-413-3

FIRST EDITION
10 9 8 7 6 5 4 3 2 1

For my daughter, Taylor Church Brigham

CONTENTS

Preface IX

CHAPTER ONE

America Goes to War 1

CHAPTER TWO

The Military Half 35

CHAPTER THREE

The Problems of Nation Building 69

CHAPTER FOUR

Staying the Course 103

CHAPTER FIVE

Challenges to America's Power 137

Acknowledgments 169

Notes 171

Index 195

PREFACE

The war in Iraq is now a major conflict, costlier in lives and treasure than any other U.S.-led war since 1975. The outcome in Iraq will have a dramatic impact on U.S. foreign policy for years and will drastically alter the geopolitical future of the Middle East.

With so much riding on the outcome in Iraq, President George W. Bush urges the nation to stay the course, arguing that America's vital national security interests are at stake. He believes there are significant signs of progress against the insurgency and the government in Baghdad grows stronger every day. He insists Iraqi forces are taking over more and more of Iraq's security needs, and the day will soon come when the United States can begin a phased withdrawal. The national elections in early 2006 and the formation of a new coalition in the prime minister's office in April 2006 are clear signs to the Bush administration that the U.S. nation-building effort is working in Iraq. Economic conditions are also improving, the president claims, further signs of progress.

Yet the war in Iraq was predicated on weapons of mass destruction that were not found and an alliance between Saddam Hussein and the al-Qaeda terrorist group that did not exist. This grim assessment of the war and its false pretexts is especially haunting because the issues raise the kind of mistakes, misjudgments, and myths that led to U.S. involvement in Vietnam. At that time, the context was the spread of communism and falling dominos in Southeast Asia. U.S. policymakers claimed Vietnam was the front line of the cold war, and the future of the free world depended upon success in that faraway place.

But is Iraq another Vietnam? Is history repeating itself? Since the first days of the U.S. invasion of Iraq, supporters of the war have cautioned the public not to view this conflict as another Vietnam. They rightfully point to several important distinctions, most involving military operations. A main purpose of this book, then, is to explore the substantial military differences between the Vietnam and Iraq wars. It is clear, from an operational and strategic standpoint, Vietnam and Iraq are very different conflicts, and the distinctions are important to make. First, in size and scope, the Vietnam War simply dwarfs the war in Iraq. Second, Vietnam began as an insurgency and escalated into a conventional war; in Iraq, the war started as a conventional invasion and deteriorated into a guerrilla war. The strategies used in both wars also differ dramatically. So, too, do the armies the United States sent into harm's way in Vietnam and Iraq. The insurgencies also share little in common, and Iraq has no charismatic figure like Ho Chi Minh to represent the civil-military movement in the public's eye. In addition, there is no air campaign over Iraq as there was in Vietnam. Perhaps the most striking difference is the geopolitical situation. The insurgents in Iraq do not have superpower backing as the

Vietnamese Communists had in their allies in Moscow and Beijing. Furthermore, outside of the Middle East, there is little if any support for the insurgents. In sharp contrast, Vietnam's National Liberation Front (NLF) enjoyed the sympathy of people in many nations, including the United States.

Yet despite the overwhelming number of differences, three similarities may be more important to the outcome in Iraq and the long-term future of U.S. foreign relations. First, in Iraq, as in Vietnam, there was no political corollary to America's overwhelming military power. The United States was never able to translate its massive firepower into a meaningful political program in Vietnam, and the same appears true in Iraq. Problems of nation building continue to plague the Bush administration in Iraq, just as they did in Vietnam for more than one U.S. administration. In an asymmetrical war, the government's ability to tackle tough social, cultural, and economic difficulties is probably more important than its ability to win and lose battles. In Iraq, as in Vietnam, the United States and its allies have been unable to win the battle for the hearts and minds of ordinary citizens. Security is a key issue, but so too is the government's ability to provide jobs, housing, and a stable economy. In Iraq today, as was the case in Vietnam, all of the key social and economic indicators point in the wrong direction. High inflation, record levels of unemployment (outside of the armed forces and national police), and lack of basic necessities threaten to destroy all that the Bush administration hopes to build. The lack of social progress and the increase in sectarian violence suggest the nation-building experiment in Iraq might meet the same fate as the twenty-year effort in Vietnam.

Another major similarity between the two conflicts is declining public support. The problem George W. Bush faces in Iraq is similar to the problem Lyndon Johnson faced in Vietnam: The public gave substantial support to the effort as troops were sent in, but that support evaporated as the war dragged on. In Vietnam, public opinion polls clearly showed that a majority of Americans supported Johnson's 1965 decisions to send combat troops to Vietnam and to give them offensive missions. Likewise, the Bush administration enjoyed enormous support from a majority of the American public when it invaded Iraq in March 2003. In each case, however, public support declined sharply in the early stages of the war because reluctant supporters were quickly alienated. By 1967 fewer than half of the American people supported the war in Vietnam, and that remained the high-water mark for the remaining eight years of war. In Iraq the drop-off has been faster than any experts predicted. Most Americans believe the perceived threats in Iraq—weapons of mass destruction and support for international terrorism—have been discounted. And most Americans simply do not share the Bush administration's enthusiasm for planting the seeds of democracy in the Middle East.

The American public's patience is wearing thin, and some quarters have already begun to pressure Congress for changes in Iraq. Congress is having a more difficult time justifying the war's cost in terms of blood and treasure, and it will not be long before the war-weary nation demands a phased withdrawal. The Bush administration, as the Johnson and Nixon administrations did before it, has launched a massive public relations campaign to drum up support for the war, but the White House and Congress probably will face growing demands to declare victory and go home. As in Vietnam, the best the Bush administration might realistically hope for is a "decent interval" between a U.S. withdrawal and a chaotic civil war in Iraq. It is impossible at this stage to predict the outcome in Iraq, but if Vietnam provides any clues—and I think it does—the road ahead looks treacherous.

At the same time, the Bush administration's increasingly aggressive stance toward Iran has begun to echo the spread of the Vietnam War into neighboring countries. In 1970 Vietnam became the focus of wider regional conflicts that extended to Laos (unofficially) and to Cambodia, with saturation bombings. To some extent, the potential for the Iraq War to be a similar key to regional embroilments has already been realized. Aggressive rhetoric for military action in Iraq has spilled over national borders. Iranian jihadists are currently operating in Iraq. Evidence already exists then, that like Vietnam, the war in Iraq has become a regional conflict.

The most important similarity between Iraq and Vietnam, however, is the challenge that each war presented to American beliefs about the use of power. In Vietnam, as in Iraq, the United States learned there were limits to what it could accomplish through force. In each war, U.S. political leaders believed in Woodrow Wilson's old adage that spreading democracy abroad would make America and the world more secure. In Vietnam, the initial goal was not simply to stop the Communists but also to build a non-Communist alternative in South Vietnam. In Iraq, the central goal was regime change. The Bush administration believed it could oust Saddam Hussein and replace him with a democratic government, which would be the first step in promoting democracy in the Middle East. Idealism and nobility of purpose, then, drove the United States to intervene in Vietnam and Iraq. Inside this idealism, however, lay the belief that the United States knew no limits to its power. To U.S. policymakers, regulating the world's political problems was not only desirable but also possible given U.S. power and will. Lyndon Johnson liked to say the reason the mantle of freedom fell to the United States was no other country had the power to lift it. George W. Bush also believed the United States was the only nation that could defend freedom in the Middle East with power and conviction.

Despite overwhelming force, technological superiority, and abundant financial resources, the United States has been incapable of coping with the enormous political complexities that inevitably emerge from protracted military conflicts. The end result might be an "Iraq syndrome" that challenges America's role in the world. After the Vietnam War, America turned inward, fearful of any military engagements outside the defense of its own borders. Interventions in the Middle East and Central America in the ensuing twenty-five years were extremely limited. Even the first Gulf War was purposefully limited in nature. Although President George H.W. Bush proclaimed the United States had in fact kicked the Vietnam syndrome with its victory in the first Gulf War, the White House knew all too well that its strategy was based on the U.S. experience in Vietnam. The goals in the first Gulf War were kept limited, there was a clear exit strategy, and the United States massed overwhelming force to meet its narrow objectives. In fact, several critics of the first Gulf War later claimed that U.S. forces should have marched all the way to Baghdad and overthrown Saddam Hussein. General Colin Powell rejected this thinking, favoring instead prudent and limited action given the U.S. experience in Vietnam.

In going to war in Iraq, the George W. Bush administration has purposefully turned its back on the lessons of Vietnam. With idealistic rhetoric, the United States has again gone out into the world in search of monsters to destroy. The difficulties the United States has experienced in Iraq, however, have forced many Americans to challenge the neoconservative agenda that led President Bush to Iraq in the first place. A growing majority of Americans no longer believe the United States should be involved in a nation-building experiment in Iraq, and fewer still support the notion of spreading democracy in the Middle East through the application of military power. The great tragedy of the Vietnam War, as might be the case in Iraq, is that the misuse of force there limited U.S. military action where it might have been required later. Hearing the echoes of Vietnam, the United States refused to intervene to stop genocide in Cambodia, the Balkans, and Rwanda before it was too late for hundreds of thousands of innocent people. Realizing the United States cannot force its will on others, the American public and Congress are now withdrawing from support of broader foreign-policy objectives. The great lesson of Vietnam and Iraq, therefore, is that the United States must use its power wisely.

CHAPTER ONE

AMERICA GOES TO WAR

T HE UNITED STATES went to war in Vietnam and Iraq with soaring rhetoric about American ideals and deep-seated fears about its security. Policymakers during the cold war and post–September 11 were responding to heightened threat perceptions that made universalisms, such as communism and terrorism, irresistible enemies. In each case, there was significant political support for military intervention because Americans believed they would be more secure with preventive strikes against their perceived enemies. Throughout American history, U.S. policymakers have responded to apparent threats by taking the offensive.[1] The attacks against Spanish Florida, the annexation of Texas, the invasion of Cuba in 1898, and the occupation of Nicaragua in the 1920s are but a few examples of this policy. The goal was always to overwhelm the sources of danger.

Another safeguard of American liberty was expansionism. Thomas Jefferson believed that expanding the country's borders provided greater national security, as did John Quincy Adams. For

Adams, safety came in the form of a continental empire, which he considered the "proper dominion" of the United States.[2] Historian Frederick Jackson Turner gave this policy a cultural and institutional grounding, suggesting democracy was born on the frontier and protected through expansion.[3] Vietnam and Iraq, then, are not aberrations. Rather, they are part of a pattern of beliefs in U.S. foreign policy grounded in the principle that it is better to strike at the enemy before it can strike at you. Preemption, if you will.

Preemptive strikes are usually explained with a nobility of purpose. In Vietnam, U.S. aid and intervention meant stopping the spread of communism, which President Dwight D. Eisenhower feared was a direct threat to liberal democracies. He believed the fall of Vietnam to Ho Chi Minh's Communists would cause "in rapid succession the collapse of the rest of Southeast Asia."[4] Eisenhower feared that if Vietnam fell, the rest of Southeast Asia would "go over very quickly," as if those countries were a "row of dominos."[5] Eisenhower also saw Ho Chi Minh as a tyrant. He believed Ho subjected his people to unusual cruelties and the Communists had the same in mind for other peoples in the region. The way to deal with tyrants, Eisenhower reasoned, was to crush them. He believed the nation had to make dictators an example for others who would challenge America's strength and security.[6] President George W. Bush shared this view. He was convinced Saddam Hussein possessed weapons of mass destruction and intended to use them on his enemies, which were considerable in number. Furthermore, Bush argued that Iraq was the nexus of an international terrorist network. In Iraq and Vietnam, the United States acted unilaterally to eliminate threats to its security. Along the way, both missions were also designed to protect others from the ravages of brutal dictatorships.

In both cases, then, the United States possessed immense power and the belief that it had to use that power to sustain America's security. The linking of power and ideals—democracy, freedom, liberty, capitalism—has not always produced the best results. Larger wars for ideals could be long on rhetoric and short on prudent judgment.[7] This certainly was the case in Vietnam, and it may be true in Iraq. In both wars, the original justification used to secure congressional authorization to begin hostile action was discredited. In each case, such action did not lead to a careful policy review. Instead, as the history of both conflicts shows, U.S. policymakers in the White House rejected carefully calibrated debates about U.S. security interests in favor of idealistic appeals for war. If Vietnam and Iraq can teach us anything about the way the United States goes to war, it is that Congress should insist on a full and frank debate before giving the president broad authority to wage war. Congress should better learn how to discipline power and harness fear.

FROM THE DOMINO THEORY
TO THE DOCTRINE OF CREDIBILITY

It was, after all, the fear of falling dominos and the lofty rhetoric about America's moral obligation to oppose communism that led to the Vietnam War. Despite the nation's enormous military power and strategic dominance, many U.S. policymakers feared the Communists could marshal greater force or be more seductive than a democratic country. Eisenhower's secretary of state, John Foster Dulles, saw the cold war in apocalyptic terms that pitted the forces of good against the forces of evil. He was convinced the United States had to combat atheistic communism with all its military might because the

Communists knew no moral law and would stop at nothing in their quest for world domination. For Dulles, Christian ideals provided the dynamic difference between success and failure in the set-piece battle against communism. He argued that the only hope of defeating the Soviets and Chinese lay in "reacting with a faith of our own." Dulles was firm in his convictions. "If history teaches us anything," he concluded, "it is that no nation is strong unless its people are imbued with a faith. . . . The impact of the dynamic upon the static . . . will always destroy what it attacks."[8]

The domino theory and a sense of messianic mission drew the United States to war in Vietnam. The conflict was not a quagmire in the 1950s but rather a noble mission in the eyes of the Eisenhower administration to save Southeast Asia from communism. U.S. leaders were so confident about the righteousness of their cause that on several occasions they failed to ask serious questions about the limits of U.S. power or the legitimacy of the domino theory. Support for the Eisenhower position in Vietnam was universal; Democrats and Republicans in both houses of Congress stood behind the domino theory. Senator John F. Kennedy, speaking before the American Friends of Vietnam in 1956, warned that Indochina "represents the cornerstone of the Free World in Southeast Asia, the keystone to the arch, the finger in the dike. Burma, Thailand, India, Japan, the Philippines and obviously Laos and Cambodia are among those whose security would be threatened if the red tide of Communism overflowed into Vietnam."[9]

So confident was the United States in its moral and military position that it rejected any political settlement to the growing crisis in Vietnam. By 1954 the French government had grown weary of its war against Ho Chi Minh's Communists for political control of Vietnam.

The French first came to Indochina in the 1850s, seeking an Asian jewel for their imperial crown. After one hundred years of colonial rule, Paris signed an armistice with the Vietnamese Communists at a conference in Geneva that promised a French withdrawal and unifying national elections in Vietnam. The Eisenhower administration rejected the Geneva accords, however, believing the United States could fare better than the French against the Communists because it was not burdened by a colonial past and because providence was on its side.[10] Accordingly, the United States presided over the birth of the Republic of Vietnam, or South Vietnam, as a counterrevolutionary alternative to Ho Chi Minh's Communists. Dulles and Eisenhower therefore linked the U.S. mission in Vietnam with American ideals. Anticommunism and the promotion of democracy along liberal lines were both a justification for war and the cornerstone of U.S. ideology.

In 1961 the new Kennedy administration engaged in a formal policy review of its options in Vietnam. Kennedy had been a longtime supporter of the domino theory and was clearly worried about Communist advances in newly developing postcolonial nations in Africa and Asia. The president and his advisers ultimately rejected the domino theory, however, believing there were situational differences in geography that could overcome politics.[11] In other words, Kennedy was less concerned about falling dominos because he no longer believed they were attached. If one nation fell to communism, that did not automatically mean neighboring countries would fall. What replaced the domino theory in Kennedy's mind, however, was his new thinking on U.S. credibility, what writer Jonathan Schell appropriately called the "psychological domino theory."[12] Kennedy believed the war in Vietnam was no longer about stopping dominos from falling but rather about showing enemies and allies the United

States lived up to its commitment "to pay any price and bear any burden" to assure "the survival and success of liberty."[13] Support of South Vietnam, not rolling back communism, became the new goal.

Perhaps Kennedy's two national security secretaries were most forceful in advocating the new policy. Secretary of State Dean Rusk often used protocols of the Southeast Asia Treaty Organization (SEATO) as sufficient reason for U.S. intervention in Vietnam. According to Rusk, provisions in the 1954 SEATO agreement demanded that the United States come to the defense of any of the signatories.[14] Since South Vietnam had signed this agreement, the United States was obligated by treaty to defend it from Communist attacks. Rusk further reasoned that if the United States did not aid South Vietnam, U.S. allies across the globe would come to doubt the U.S. commitment to its treaty obligations. Rusk was particularly worried that U.S. allies in NATO would wonder if Washington would stand behind that agreement should the Soviets invade another country in Europe. Secretary of Defense Robert S. McNamara argued that if the United States did not intervene in Vietnam, both sides of the Iron Curtain would sense "a major crisis of nerve."[15] In a report to the president, McNamara concluded that "the loss of South Vietnam would . . . undermine the credibility of American commitments elsewhere."[16] By 1961, according to historian Fred Logevall, the doctrine of credibility had "supplanted the domino theory in American thinking on Vietnam."[17]

LIMITED-WAR THEORY

This change in rationale also brought with it a change in strategic thinking. Throughout the Eisenhower years, U.S. foreign policy was based on the concept of mutually assured destruction (called MAD). The president believed if he built up the U.S. nuclear arsenal so that it could withstand a first strike from the Soviets, this would deter Moscow from aggressive action. Although the "New Look," as Eisenhower's policy was called, did keep the United States out of major confrontation with the Soviets, it also limited the president's options. Kennedy argued he needed a more flexible policy—one that more accurately reflected the needs of an administration willing to meet the Soviet threat anywhere around the globe. Kennedy envisioned a strategy that would allow the United States to act quickly and decisively against Communists in the jungles of Southeast Asia and on the plains in Africa.[18] However, Kennedy did not want these confrontations to lead to a nuclear exchange with the Soviets. Any local war with a country inside the fraternal socialist world system risked a larger war with China or the Soviet Union. Since the Soviet Union possessed nuclear weapons, the balance of terror limited U.S. policymakers in their actions.

At the time, most foreign-affairs decisions were seen through the prism of the cold war and the limitations it presented. The primary national security issue of the era was preventing a catastrophic war that might well escalate into a nuclear war with the Soviet Union. The Kennedy administration balanced the need to confront Soviet meddling in newly emerging postcolonial nations with the need to avoid a nuclear exchange with the Communist camp through what it called "limited-war theory."

The product of American academics Robert Osgood, Thomas Schelling, and Herman Kahn, limited-war theory gave the president a way to keep wars local and thereby avoid a nuclear showdown.[19] At the heart of this new doctrine was the belief that the president should have the option to respond to Soviet aggression at a low level of violence or through diplomacy. The president could move up the rungs of a ladder of escalation, until such time as the enemy chose to cease and desist its activities rather than face the consequences of further escalation.[20] With enough applied military pressure, according to the theory, the president could communicate to the enemy that it would pay a high price if aggression continued. In the case of Vietnam, the goal was to convince Hanoi that continuing to support revolution in the south would come at too high a price. Each military escalation, therefore, was a signal to Hanoi to cease and desist. Of course, Hanoi rejected Washington's signals, matching each military escalation with its own.[21]

U.S. fears were not limited to Moscow's cold-war power or influence. China was a legitimate threat to U.S. troops in Vietnam. McNamara was convinced during the war that invading North Vietnam with U.S. ground forces carried with it unacceptable risks.[22] He correctly concluded China would act in its own self-interest and would consider any attack across the seventeenth parallel that divided North Vietnam from South Vietnam an attack against its own borders.[23] General Bruce Palmer, General William Westmoreland's deputy in Vietnam, agreed. He argued in his book *The Twenty-five-Year War* that "one cannot quarrel with the decision not to invade North Vietnam because it was too close to China."[24] U.S. officials now know North Vietnam asked for and received security commitments from Beijing from 1960 onward.[25] They also know China's Seventh Air Force was moved permanently to the Vietnamese border in case of a ground attack across the seventeenth parallel.[26] Four other air divisions were also moved closer to the border, and Beijing built two airstrips near Lang Son in anticipation of a U.S. invasion.[27]

By 1968 over 200,000 Chinese troops were serving within North Vietnam's borders.[28]

Kennedy changed not only the rationale for war but also its strategic doctrine. In rejecting the domino theory in favor of the theory of credibility in the struggle against international communism, the president was willing to give up North Vietnam to protect South Vietnam. He was also willing to limit the U.S. military commitment to Vietnam to avoid a larger war that might entice China and the Soviet Union to join the conflict. The second-order issue—protecting South Vietnam from a Communist takeover through the application of limited U.S. military pressure—proved more difficult to accomplish than anyone in the Kennedy administration had originally thought. The South Vietnamese government of President Ngo Dinh Diem was corrupt, inefficient, and not very democratic. Diem did little to reach out to those who were in the minority view on some issues.[29] He persecuted Buddhists, believing they were sympathetic to the Communist cause; he rejected land reform programs supported by the United States; and he closed down newspapers that were critical of his rule.[30]

EXPANSION OR WITHDRAWAL?

By the middle of 1963, a frustrated John F. Kennedy was considering another major policy revision. First on Kennedy's list of things to change in Vietnam was President Diem. Despite some support in his administration for staying the course with Diem and his brother, Ngo Dinh Nhu, there was overwhelming backing for regime change in Saigon.[31] Many Kennedy officials believed the U.S. counterinsurgency war was doomed with Diem at the helm.[32] Others argued the

Prez
Diem + Brother by own officers
Assass in Back.
10   IS IRAQ ANOTHER VIETNAM?

political war so essential to victory was being lost every day because Diem cared little for the village war or for peasants caught in the conflict.[33] What Kennedy envisioned for Diem is still debatable; perhaps he believed the South Vietnamese president would be replaced in a bloodless coup. In the end, however, Diem's own officers executed him and his brother in the back of an armored personnel carrier.

After Diem's assassination, events in Saigon spun out of control. Various political groups wrestled for power in the capital, and the Communists made significant advances in the countryside. In fact, the Communist Party hoped to take advantage of the chaos in Saigon. At its December 1963 plenum, party leaders agreed to "escalate the level of armed struggle in the South."[34] According to party leaders, "armed struggle would be the direct and deciding factor in the annihilation of the armed forces of the enemy."[35] Le Duan, the party's secretary general and a longtime advocate of a more forceful military policy in South Vietnam, applauded the decision.

As Hanoi turned up the heat, the Kennedy administration considered its options. One option was to withdraw. Convinced South Vietnam would eventually "throw our asses out," and needing to score some political points without a huge military cost, Kennedy had considered a limited withdrawal as early as 1962.[36] By April 1963, some administration officials suggested that withdrawing 1,000 U.S. advisers "out of the blue" would reassure the American public the war was going well and undercut the Communists' "best propaganda line" that the United States was running the war for South Vietnam.[37] Kennedy had McNamara draw up the plans for the limited withdrawal to begin in December 1963. Many believed the president was starting to phase down U.S. operations in Vietnam, and that after the 1964 presidential election he would withdraw all U.S. troops.

McNamara went on record stating he was convinced Kennedy would have withdrawn U.S. forces had he been reelected.[38] No one will ever know. Kennedy was assassinated November 22, 1963.

Of course, Kennedy had another option, which was to intervene more forcefully. With just over 16,000 U.S. advisers in Vietnam, it was clear more could be done to prop up the Saigon government and to aid the South Vietnamese armed forces. From the earliest days of the administration, some of Kennedy's key advisers had advocated a more militant line.[39] By summer 1963 many were calling for the president to introduce U.S. ground troops to take over the war from the South Vietnamese forces and to save Saigon from total defeat.[40] Others suggested a strong air campaign over North Vietnam would take some pressure off South Vietnam.[41] It now seems clear Kennedy refused to ask the hard questions about U.S. intervention in Vietnam, content instead to continue to steer a middle course that promised neither withdrawal nor greater involvement.

When Lyndon Johnson entered the Oval Office, he, too, could have expanded the war or withdrawn. In typical Johnson fashion, he chose neither course. Always wanting to keep his options open, Johnson usually took the path that limited his policy choices. The president and his national security advisers decided to continue Kennedy's commitment to the defense of South Vietnam and to keep America's role in the war limited. On March 17, 1964, Johnson outlined his decision in what is now known as National Security Memorandum No. 288.[42] Expanding on Kennedy's redefinition of the war's aims, Johnson argued that nothing short of U.S. credibility was at stake in Vietnam. The administration would continue to support South Vietnam in its hour of need, the president concluded, because the United States was the only power that could do so. In the face of danger, the

United States never backed down. Rusk perhaps put it best when he argued that the "integrity of the U.S. commitment is the principal pillar of peace throughout the world. If that commitment becomes unreliable, the communist world would draw conclusions that would lead to our ruin and almost certainly to a catastrophic war."[43] America's war aims in Vietnam during the Johnson years were still focused on containment and credibility.

Thus, U.S. goals in the Kennedy and Johnson years were counterrevolutionary. First, the United States wanted to stop the spread of communism in Southeast Asia, and then after rejecting the domino theory, U.S. policymakers wanted to stop the Communists from taking over South Vietnam. As the war dragged on, the chief goal became convincing enemies and allies alike that the United States honored its treaty commitments. Credibility was as important as the specific military mission. Containment, preservation, and credibility were the hallmarks of America's war aims in Vietnam. Only in building up South Vietnam as a viable alternative to Ho Chi Minh's Communists did the United States move from the defensive to the offensive.

THE BUILDUP TO IRAQ: FROM WEAPONS OF MASS DESTRUCTION TO THE WAR ON TERROR

The Iraq War, in sharp contrast, is revolutionary. U.S. war aims include effecting regime change, spreading democracy in the region, and destroying an international terrorist network. The rationale for such a radical agenda began in early 2003, when Colin Powell, then Bush's secretary of state, appeared before the United Nations (UN).

Powell argued that Saddam Hussein was taunting the United Nations and its various resolutions urging him to comply with weapons inspections.[44] If the UN was to have any relevance, Powell argued, it needed to pass a Security Council resolution authorizing military strikes against Iraq, as it had done in the first Gulf War (1990–1991). Short of that, Powell warned, the United States was prepared to go it alone because its strength was beyond challenge and there was a monster out there to destroy. According to Powell, Hussein was developing weapons of mass destruction to "project power, to threaten, and to deliver chemical, biological and, if we let him, nuclear warheads."[45] He also indicated that a second-order issue for the Bush administration was a "sinister nexus between Iraq and the Al Qaeda terrorist network, a nexus that combines classic terrorist organizations and modern methods of murder."[46]

For nearly a year before Powell's UN speech, President George W. Bush was delivering the same message. In 2002 he argued the United States had a responsibility to change the course of events in Iraq because the threat from that country "stands alone" and because it "gathers the most serious dangers of our age in one place."[47] When no weapons of mass destruction were found in Iraq following the March 2003 invasion, the Bush administration shifted its war rationale completely to the war on terror and promoting democracy in the region. Bush and his national security team have since argued that the insurgency in Iraq is led by Osama bin Laden and his Jordanian subcontractor Abu Musab al-Zarqawi. They suggest the only factor keeping the insurgency alive is the cross-border invasion of Iraq by these radical elements. Despite the growing evidence that much of the insurgency is directed by Sunni rebels inside Iraq and by Shiites in certain strongholds, like Muqtada al-Sadr's Mahdi army in Najaf, the Bush administration continues to make the connection between events in Iraq and the al-Qaeda network.

THE BUSH DOCTRINE AND THE NEOCONS

The war on terror was spelled out specifically in what is now known as the Bush Doctrine. Originally outlined in the president's graduation address in June 2002 at West Point, the Bush Doctrine was formally delineated in the president's report on *The National Security Strategy of the United States of America* (NSS), released September 17, 2002.[48] In this document, the Bush administration outlined its ambitious and comprehensive grand strategy: "We will defend the peace by fighting terrorists and tyrants. We will preserve the peace by building good relations among the great powers. We will extend the peace by encouraging free and open societies on every continent."[49] The Bush Doctrine also pledges that the United States "will identify and eliminate terrorists wherever they are, together with the regimes that sustain them."[50] Following the direction of nineteenth-century U.S. leaders, Bush pledged to launch preemptive strikes against the enemy before its forces could attack the United States. Unlike most other presidents, with the exception of Franklin Roosevelt and James Madison, however, Bush had tangible evidence of the destructive capacity of America's enemies if left unchallenged.

Given the president's strategy to attack America's enemies first, what propelled the Bush administration to invade Iraq? In many ways, Iraq was the most secular country in the region, and not one terrorist from the September 11 attacks was an Iraqi. Still, Bush found compelling reasons for Iraq to put the Bush Doctrine in action. An attack against Iraq could topple a tyrant, showing the rest of the world the United States would not sit by and watch evil wield power. By defeating Saddam sufficiently, the Bush administration hoped to shatter the dreams of others who wished the United States harm. An attack against Iraq could also finish the job started in the first Gulf War, when the United States launched a counterattack against Saddam to force him to exit Kuwait. Some have suggested President Bush was highly influenced by Elliot Cohen's book *Supreme Command*, which was critical of George H.W. Bush (Bush I) for not taking Baghdad at the end of the first Gulf War.[51] Attacking Iraq also promised to root out the terrorists whom Bush believed Saddam had been supporting all along.

At the core of the Bush administration's rationale for invading Iraq lay also the belief that the United States needed to attack the conditions that had led to the rise of terrorists. Bush and his closest advisers believed the nation needed to promote democracy in the Middle East because it was the very lack of representative institutions within Arab societies that drove terrorists to drastic measures. The attacks of September 11 were led by middle-class, relatively well educated men who came from countries with no democratic traditions, Bush reasoned, and therefore they had no outlet for their political grievances. Starting with Iraq, the United States would plant the seeds of democracy and watch them grow. For Bush, democracy itself was a transformative power, and its expansion in the Middle East promised to make the United States more secure. With new democratic institutions, the Arab middle class would take ownership of the political process alongside the traditional royal families and authoritarian regimes. Shared power through a more democratic state, Bush believed, could transform the Middle East from an unpredictable and

[handwritten: Paul Wolfowitz Chief Architect of Bush's policy]

[handwritten margin note: Wolfowitz ↓]

potentially dangerous region into a stable and peaceful one. The Bush administration firmly believed history was on the side of democratic states and Washington had an obligation to use its considerable power to bring about democratic change.

The chief architect of this policy was Paul Wolfowitz, Bush's former deputy secretary of defense. Wolfowitz had a long and distinguished career in government before joining the Bush administration, first working for U.S. Senator Henry "Scoop" Jackson (D-Wash.) as an aide and later with Fred Ikle, director of the U.S. Arms Control and Disarmament Agency. In the latter post, Wolfowitz became one the most important members of "Team B," a committee designed to assess the Soviet threat. Team B challenged many of Henry Kissinger's beliefs about Soviet intentions and capabilities, suggesting the U.S. policy of détente had distracted American policymakers from Moscow's "darker side."[52] During the Carter years, Wolfowitz moved to the Pentagon where he would return after a Clinton-era sabbatical as dean of the Paul Nitze School at Johns Hopkins University and as ambassador to Indonesia. He became Bush's deputy secretary for defense in 2001. *[handwritten: Neocons —   1930's NY]*

Many of Wolfowitz's ideas came from neoconservative thinking that had developed over the course of the twentieth century. This neoconservatism took root among a small group of intellectuals, based mainly in New York in the late 1930s. That group included Irving Kristol, Daniel Bell, Irving Howe, and Nathan Glazer. Early in their adult lives, these young men were attracted to the writings of Leon Trotsky. They believed in social progress and the universality of rights but feared that communism under Stalin had grown excessive. Over time, they grew more critical of communism in general. By the late 1940s, their ideas were cemented around the belief that all totalitarian regimes would crumble if pushed hard enough. In 1989 and 1991, the neoconservatives celebrated the end of the cold war and the collapse of the Soviet Union. In their book *Present Dangers,* two leading neoconservatives, William Kristol and Robert Kagan, argued that the victory over the Soviets and the Eastern bloc could be repeated if the United States was willing to add muscle to its foreign policy. They wrote, "To many the idea of America using its power to promote changes of regimes in nations ruled by dictators rings of utopianism. But in fact, it is eminently realistic. There is something perverse in declaring the impossibility of promoting democratic change abroad in light of the record of the past three decades."[53] Wolfowitz believed regime change was possible in Iraq following Kristol and Kagan's logic. He also supported the neoconservative idea that there was a universal hunger for liberty in all people and they would rise up to support democratic challenges to dictatorial regimes.

After the September 11 attacks, therefore, Wolfowitz called on the Bush administration to launch preemptive strikes against Iraq as well as intervene directly in Afghanistan.[54] He also suggested the global war against terror be seen as a global war for freedom.[55] Liberating Iraq would be the first step in democratizing the Middle East. Since the Arab Street respects force, Wolfowitz reasoned, the U.S. should link its power with its mission. He knowingly committed the United States to a broader and heavily militarized strategy of liberating the entire Islamic world. Unlike in Vietnam, the dominos would fall in the Middle East—but in the opposite direction. After Iraq, the rest of the Middle East would be up for grabs. These radical ideas remain the cornerstone of the Bush administration's policy in Iraq, even though Wolfowitz has since left the Pentagon to become president of the World Bank.

World Band Pree - Wolfow.tz

Jefferson

EXPORTING AMERICAN IDEALS

In many ways, the Bush administration is following another impulse in U.S. foreign policy—the belief that exporting democracy makes America more secure. This idea has deep historical roots. Jefferson called the expansion of U.S. ideals essential for the survival of the "empire of liberty."[56] He saw no contradiction between the creation of an empire and liberty. He believed an expanding liberal empire was actually the best safeguard of liberty. Woodrow Wilson called it making the world safe for democracy.[57] Inside Wilson's liberalism was the belief that autocrats, like the German kaiser, had wrestled freedom from their people. Once these autocrats were destroyed, the people could create liberal, democratic governments. These principles lay behind Wilson's willingness to take the nation to war in Europe, even though most Americans saw it as conflict between competing imperial empires that need not affect the United States. Wilson saw it differently. He believed the peace following such a war held the potential to create a new world order. From the ashes of old Europe, the United States could rebuild the international community on American principles.[58] For Wilson, then, free people would naturally want American democracy. It was his obligation to give it to them.

Lyndon Johnson also believed in exporting American ideals. Where George W. Bush has envisioned new democratic institutions to harness anger and frustration abroad, Johnson saw access to resources and economic opportunity as the keys to security and stability. As a young U.S. senator, Johnson had supported Franklin Roosevelt's New Deal programs, believing the government had a responsibility to end poverty and want. He had an emotional attachment to the New Deal and its liberal philosophy, because as a young man in Texas, he had seen what Roosevelt's program could do. He was particularly attracted to the programs of the Tennessee Valley Authority (TVA), which dammed rivers and lakes to provide electricity to the deep South. "Where I live," Johnson was fond of saying, "I have seen the night illuminated, and the kitchen warmed, and the home heated, where once the cheerless night and the ceaseless cold held sway. And all this happened because electricity came to our area along the humming wires of the REA [Rural Electrification Administration], a part of the TVA."[59]

In Vietnam, Johnson believed it was his responsibility to do more than simply stop the spread of communism. He also believed it was essential to show that what had worked for America during the 1930s depression would work in Vietnam. Johnson argued the United States had the "power" and the "opportunity" to "improve the life of man in that conflict-torn corner of the world."[60] In a speech at Johns Hopkins University in April 1965, one month after the first U.S. ground troops landed in Vietnam, Johnson promised the war could end tomorrow if only Hanoi would embrace Johnson's liberal philosophy in an effort to help its own people the way the New Deal had helped Americans. The president offered that the United States was ready to help the Vietnamese overcome "the bondage of material misery" if they would only put the war aside.[61] The United States could be a force for great economic change in Vietnam, if only Ho would let it.

The cornerstone of Johnson's New Deal for Vietnam was a bold economic development plan along the lines of the Tennessee Valley Authority. Johnson pledged $1 billion to create a Mekong River Development Project that would harness that mighty river's power to bring cheap electricity and economic development to Vietnam.[62] "Old Ho can't turn me down," Johnson told aide Bill Moyers after the former's proposal was carried on nationwide television.[63] For Johnson, the promise of government had always been its transformative powers. In the area of foreign relations, the inexperienced Johnson saw everything through the eyes of that Texas boy who marveled at the light. He wanted to "leave the footprints of America in Vietnam," and held the lasting belief that "when Americans come, this is what they leave—schools, not long cigars. We're going to turn the Mekong into a Tennessee Valley."[64]

For Johnson, exporting the best of what America had to offer was the answer to the most pressing problems in Vietnam. The same premise holds for Bush's efforts in Iraq. But as both men were to discover, that war aim proved elusive. Three years into the nation-building experiment in Iraq, there seemed to be sufficient evidence that terrorism did not originate from the absence of democracy alone. It may be that the very values Bush is trying to export remain a primary target for most terrorists, as Samuel Huntington has argued.[65] Or, it may be that ethnic, religious, and tribal differences *within* Iraq are the source of violence. The conflict may not be a clash of civilizations, but rather, as John Lewis Gaddis and others have noted, it may be a clash within a civilization that fuels the fire of hatred.[66] Is the Islamic world struggling with itself to determine what kind of future it wants? Is there such a thing as the Islamic world? In other words, is it possible to say that all Arab countries or organizations see the political future of the region in the same way? With such uncertainties, it is no wonder the Bush administration has had a tough go of it in Iraq.

For Lyndon Johnson, giving the Mekong Delta a New Deal–style face-lift was equally problematic. The Communists ignored his pleas to consider economic growth and development instead of war. Johnson, hopelessly out of touch with the realities of rural Vietnam, believed everyone worldwide would embrace his New Deal. When Hanoi rejected his overtures, Johnson was crushed. He reportedly told aide Jack Valenti that Ho was out of his mind for choosing bombs over economic development. "My God, I've offered Ho Chi Minh $100 million to build a Mekong Valley. If that'd been George Meany, he'd have snapped at it!"[67] The Communists turned their back on the one thing that Johnson knew worked: government-funded economic development programs. Johnson's hope of channeling the radical Vietnamese revolution along liberal New Deal lines was further evidence of the huge cultural gap between the United States and Vietnam. National liberation, not economic development along capitalist lines, was the primary goal of the Vietnamese revolution. Eventually, Johnson's own allies in Saigon would spurn similar projects. The president left the White House in 1969 still wondering why the Vietnamese did not grasp the significance of his offer. For Johnson, Hanoi's refusal to cooperate with him on a New Deal for Vietnam left him few options.

Whether seeking to expand the security of American institutions by spreading them abroad, or using such ideals as a cover for aggression, neither Bush nor Johnson took the United States to a war footing alone. Congress agreed in both cases to give the president unbridled authority to wage war without declaring it. Members of Congress in both houses overwhelmingly supported the two presidents' war aims and agreed the missions in Vietnam and Iraq were worth American blood and treasure.

PREPARING THE COUNTRY FOR WAR IN VIETNAM

In August 1964, Congress gave Lyndon Johnson broad presidential authority to use any means necessary to put down Communist aggression in Vietnam.[68] The Congress was responding to claims by the Johnson administration that North Vietnamese torpedo boats had fired on U.S. destroyers patrolling international waters. On the afternoon of August 2, 1964, the destroyer USS *Maddox* was on a secret mission in the Tonkin Gulf, near North Vietnam's coastline. The *Maddox* was part of a larger flotilla that had launched attacks against the nearby island of Hon Me. South Vietnamese gunboats had launched the attacks in part to see how North Vietnam would respond. They found out soon enough as North Vietnamese torpedo boats attacked the *Maddox*. After a brief exchange of fire, the torpedo boats were driven away.[69]

News of the attacks enraged Johnson, but he ordered no new retaliation. Instead, Johnson agreed with the Joint Chiefs of Staff who argued that the *Maddox* should resume its operations in the Gulf of Tonkin. The navy also ordered another destroyer, the *C. Turner Joy*, to the gulf to support the *Maddox*. The administration kept the destroyers near the North Vietnamese coast, hoping to draw the Communists into another exchange. According to historian George C. Herring, some military officials were so eager to go to war against North Vietnam that they "were choosing targets for retaliatory raids before reports of a second attack began to come in."[70] They soon got their wish. On the night of August 4, while operating in heavy seas sixty miles off the North Vietnamese coast, the *Maddox* and the *Turner Joy* reported new attacks. Sonar and radar reports confirmed North Vietnamese gunboats were in the area and had fired torpedoes.[71]

Almost immediately, key members of the Johnson administration called for swift and decisive action against North Vietnam. McNamara argued the United States could not "sit still as a nation and let them attack us on the high seas and get away with it."[72] Dean Rusk believed that if the United States did not respond with considerable force, the world would think it was a "paper tiger."[73] The Joint Chiefs insisted Johnson respond immediately with retaliatory air strikes aimed at the heart of North Vietnam's war production facilities and naval shipyards.[74]

Only the Central Intelligence Agency (CIA) urged caution, suggesting Hanoi might have been acting out of pride and defensively to the raids on Hon Me island.[75] Johnson dismissed the CIA's argument, opting instead for a "firm, swift retaliatory strike" against North Vietnamese torpedo bases and oil storage dumps.[76]

Ignoring new evidence brought forward on the afternoon of August 4, which suggested a second attack had not occurred, Johnson accepted the recommendation of the commander in chief of the Pacific fleet, Admiral U.S. Grant Sharp, to launch the attack.[77] By that evening, U.S. air strikes had destroyed twenty-five North Vietnamese patrol boats and an oil storage facility in Ho Chi Minh's hometown of Vinh. Johnson went on nationwide television to tell the American people of the North Vietnamese attacks and the U.S. response. The president recounted the events of the past two days, stating that hostile North Vietnamese actions against the *Maddox* and the *C. Turner Joy* had forced him "to order the military forces of the United States to take action in reply."[78] Johnson concluded his remarks by assuring his listeners the United States was right to respond with strength. "Firmness in the right is indispensable today for peace. That firmness will always be measured. Its mission is peace."[79]

Thirty years later in Hanoi, I sat next to Robert S. McNamara and General Vo Nguyen Giap when the Vietnamese military leader told Johnson's secretary of defense that no second attack had occurred. McNamara was convinced by Giap's explanation and included that exchange in his lessons on how to avoid conflict in the future.[80] It now seems clear no second attack did occur, even though it is doubt-ful McNamara purposefully deceived the president. More likely, an administration itching for war took limited intelligence information as a clear sign of aggression because that was what it wanted all along. For months, the Johnson administration had been exploring its options in Vietnam, hoping to find some way to save South Viet-nam from complete collapse. The coup against Diem in November 1963 had created chaos in Saigon, and the Communists had increased their military pressure to deal a deathblow to South Vietnam. By summer 1964 several key members of the Johnson administration favored a direct attack against North Vietnam to save South Viet-nam.[81] The Gulf of Tonkin attacks, therefore, came at a favorable time and provided the pretext for a larger war.

Following his television address, Johnson asked Congress for a res-olution that gave him full power to respond to the Communists in Vietnam. The resolution authorized the president to take "all neces-sary measures to repel any armed attacks against the forces of the United States and to prevent further aggression."[82] Short of a declara-tion of war, the Tonkin Gulf Resolution united the nation behind more aggressive action in Vietnam. With limited debate, in fewer than ten hours, the U.S. Senate overwhelmingly approved the measure. Only Senators Wayne Morse (D-Ore.) and Ernest Gruening (D-Alaska) voted against the resolution. In the House, the debate lasted an unbe-lievably brief forty minutes, and the measure passed unanimously.[83]

Many members of Congress beat the war drum along with John-son. Ross Adair, a Republican congressman from Indiana, claimed "the American flag had been fired upon." He declared the United States "cannot tolerate such things."[84] Senator J. William Fulbright (D-Ark.), chair of the Senate Foreign Relations Committee, agreed.

The skillful senator steered Johnson's resolution through Congress, stressing the Senate's patriotic duty and the president's caution. He urged his colleagues to think of the resolution as a moderate measure "calculated to prevent the spread of war."[85] He argued that the president would consult Congress before enlarging the war, and assured his fellow senators "no one wanted another land war in Asia."[86] Fulbright also reminded his colleagues it was an election year, and the Democratic-controlled Congress did not want to spar with their party's president shortly before national elections.

Johnson was pleased with the broad authority given to him by Congress. "Like grandma's nightshirt," he later joked, "it covered everything."[87] Overnight the president's approval ratings went up 30 percent.[88] Congress and the American public had spoken. They supported the president, his war aims, and his belief that the United States would be more secure with limited but strategic attacks on the Communists. Drawing on earlier U.S. formulations of preemption and expansion, the Johnson administration took the nation to war in Vietnam to protect its perceived interests, its ideals, and its borders. The common impulse in U.S. foreign relations to strike out against an adversary before it could strike at the nation overwhelmed any potential debate inside the administration, in the Congress, or among the American people. As Johnson went to war, he had expanded presidential power and the full support of the vast majority of the American public. The same was true for George W. Bush.

THE RUSH TO WAR IN IRAQ

Shortly before Colin Powell's testimony at the United Nations in February 2003, the Bush administration moved quickly to gain support for its war aims, in Congress and with the American people. On September 4, 2002, Bush sent a letter to key members of Congress suggesting he would soon seek that body's support for action in Iraq. The president said he needed to consult with Congress to figure out "how to disarm an outlaw regime."[89] Bush maintained that following the first Gulf War, Saddam Hussein remained a "threat to peace."[90] Particularly upsetting to Bush was Hussein's refusal to cooperate with UN weapons inspectors. According to the president, Baghdad had defied at least sixteen UN resolutions. Bush suggested Iraq was hiding something, and it was up to the United States to find out what that was. He feared Hussein was seeking weapons of mass destruction to use against the United States and Israel as he had against his own people. The president pledged his administration's cooperation with Congress as it held hearings to come to terms with Iraq.

During those hearings, Bush officials focused on two key items: weapons of mass destruction and Iraq's support of terrorists. The president's key advisers testified that Saddam Hussein had used lethal gas against his own people and that he was obviously developing new weapons to use against the United States and Israel. Furthermore, the administration claimed, Iraq was now harboring an international terrorist network that included many members of Osama bin Laden's al-Qaeda team. Although the evidence to support such claims was shaky at best, administration officials testified the president believed Iraq was now a direct threat to the security of the United States. Some members of Congress balked at the administration's claims, but most were convinced by the president's message.

Eventually, Congress gave the president the war resolution he had been seeking. On October 9, 2002, both houses of Congress passed

HJ114, authorizing the president to "use the Armed Forces of the United States as he determines to be necessary and appropriate in order to defend the national security of the United States against the continued threat posed by Iraq" and to "enforce all relevant United Nations Security Council resolutions regarding Iraq."[91] Careful not to give Bush a blank check in Iraq, Congress did place limits on the president's actions. The resolution required the president to consult Congress within forty-eight hours of taking direct military action in Iraq and to report on the war's progress to the appropriate congressional committees every sixty days.[92] Like Johnson before him, President Bush received bipartisan support for the war resolution. Key Democrats voted in favor of the resolution, including Senator John Kerry, Bush's 2004 presidential election opponent from Massachusetts. Most members of Congress believed, as Senator John McCain (R-Ariz.) did, that the president's team made "a convincing case" against Iraq. Tom DeLay, Republican leader of the House, concluded during the congressional debate that "military action is inevitable."[93]

A small minority in Congress opposed the resolution. Senator Robert Byrd (D–W.Va.) argued it gave the president "unchecked authority." Senator Edward Kennedy (D-Mass.) concluded that only Congress could declare war. He worried Congress was giving the president too much power for war in advance. Few of the protests concerned the invasion itself. Most looked to the constitutional issue as Byrd and Kennedy had done. Richard Gephardt, one of the authors of the resolution, had once been a Democratic presidential hopeful.[94] By fall 2002 he was helping a Republican president gain broad war powers from Congress. Senate minority leader Tom Daschle (D–S.Dak.), a Vietnam veteran and usually outspoken critic of the Bush administration, also supported the measure.[95] In the end, the Senate passed the House version of the resolution without changing a single word.

The congressional resolution safely tucked in his pocket, President Bush then went to the American people to gain their support. In his most important public speech on Iraq, his State of the Union address on January 28, 2003, President Bush gave his first hard evidence that Iraq was trying to obtain weapons of mass destruction. In what is now referred to as the "infamous 16 words," Bush declared, "The British government has learned that Saddam Hussein recently sought significant quantities of uranium from Africa."[96] For the first time, Bush made the connection between Iraq and weapons of mass destruction. Furthermore, Bush also made a convincing argument that Iraq had harbored terrorists since the ending of the first Gulf War. With successful strikes in Afghanistan against key terrorist networks in 2002, many of America's sworn enemies were now operating inside Iraq, according to Bush, with Saddam Hussein's support and approval. In public opinion polls across the United States following the speech, an overwhelming majority of the American people favored a direct strike against Iraq before it could attack the United States.[97]

With Congress and the American public on board, Bush moved to secure support from the United Nations and the international community. Powell's speech before the UN in February 2003 was designed to produce a Security Council resolution against Iraq much like the one used to justify coalition attacks against Baghdad in the first Gulf War. When the Security Council refused to adopt such a resolution, Secretary of Defense Donald Rumsfeld suggested the United States did not need "old Europe" to defend its interests, a thinly veiled attack on the French who opposed the UN resolution forcefully.[98] Of the major U.S. allies, only Britain's Tony Blair supported the United States and its desire for regime change in Iraq.

In short, by the time of the March 2003 invasion of Iraq, the Bush administration had a congressional resolution authorizing the attack, a major ally by its side, and the support of the American people.

Just as in Vietnam, however, the rush to war had precluded significant debate. With the resolution vote held just one month before the 2002 midterm elections, few members of Congress wanted to openly challenge the president and the majority party. Furthermore, just as in Vietnam, the major reason for action turned out to be quickly discredited. There was no provocative second attack in the Tonkin Gulf, and there were no weapons of mass destruction in Iraq. Even the one piece of hard evidence the Bush administration offered to link Baghdad with nuclear weapons vanished when it was discovered that the British report making the connection between Iraq and a source of uranium in Africa was fabricated. Both wars thus were built on intelligence failures and misreading of important security information. More important, however, in Vietnam and Iraq, both presidents had the support of Congress as they marched to war.

THE EMPHASIS ON RHETORIC OVER DEBATE

Vietnam and Iraq were not the first attempts by the president to use a congressional fig leaf for waging war. In 1798, John Adams used executive power to maneuver the United States toward an undeclared war with France. James Madison used presidential authority to subvert and then seize western Florida in what some historians have called the earliest analogue to the Gulf of Tonkin Resolution.[99] James K. Polk asked Congress for a declaration of war against Mexico after he forced a military confrontation. Yet Vietnam and Iraq clearly illustrate the changing nature of the relationship between Congress and the president in the context of war. Even after experiencing Vietnam and the growing power of the presidency, Congress nevertheless repealed the War Powers Act and restored unusual authority to the president. The main problem in Iraq, as in Vietnam, was that it was relatively easy for the president to speak to ideals and not interests when laying out his war plan before Congress and the American people. Heightened threat perceptions and the uniquely American impulse to strike out against potential adversaries led the United States to war in Iraq and Vietnam. In both wars, fear and the appeal to ideals all but completely quashed debate. It is remarkable that so few members of Congress have called for a policy review in Iraq, especially given the changing nature of U.S. war aims.

The similarities in how the United States went to war in Vietnam and Iraq should prompt Americans to be more critical when reviewing the rationale for war. It is impossible for the public to know the intelligence variables that factor into a decision about war, but history does suggest that grand rhetoric and a strong appeal to ideals are no substitute for prudent judgment and careful planning. Nor is there much historical evidence to suggest that expansionism and preemption have delivered peace and security to the American people. In the early nineteenth century, John Quincy Adams believed expansion across the continent promised to make Americans safe from most potential enemies. President James K. Polk increased U.S. territory by 50 percent hoping to make Americans more secure and their institutions the envy of all. Woodrow Wilson, like Presidents Lyndon Johnson and George W. Bush, believed the United States had a moral obligation to spread its blessings to the rest of the world. In Iraq, as in Vietnam, the United States met enemies who rejected not only that line of thinking but also perhaps even the very institutions and way of life Washington was trying to project.

In both Iraq and Vietnam, the United States went to war under the cloud of insecurity. Fearful that communism was on the march or that terrorists might strike at any moment, U.S. policymakers adopted exalted rhetoric to convince ordinary Americans that national security issues were at stake. Preemption and expansion promised to eliminate threats and make the world a more stable place. In this sense, Iraq and Vietnam are clearly in the U.S. foreign-policy tradition. Like other conflicts before them, these two wars emphasized threat and security for their rationale. The United States needed to launch preemptive—and, if need be, unilateral—strikes against perceived enemies who threatened American security and ideals. Unlike most previous wars, however, those original threats were largely discredited well before either war ended. The cause of great fear and insecurity simply was not there.

This development shifted U.S. war aims in both Iraq and Vietnam, but it did not lead to a full policy review. After the Kennedy administration rejected the domino theory, it did not go to Congress and admit North Vietnam was no longer a threat to the entire region or to the United States directly. Saving South Vietnam and maintaining U.S. credibility replaced saving all of Southeast Asia from communism. In Iraq, there are no weapons of mass destruction and there remains little evidence to connect Saddam Hussein to al-Qaeda. It also seems clear the Bush administration has backed away from its original goal of spreading democracy in the Middle East, especially after the Hamas militant group posted a surprise victory in the January 2006 Palestinian election.

Clearly, the White House and Congress should have debated the war resolutions for Vietnam and Iraq more forcefully. In both cases, a debate daily for a full month or more would not have jeopardized U.S. security or national interests. Instead of debate measured in hours, wisdom and hindsight teach that days and weeks are perhaps the better metric. Indeed, the Senate debated making Martin Luther King's birthday a national holiday two weeks longer than it debated either the Gulf of Tonkin Resolution or the resolution authorizing the Bush administration to invade Iraq.[100] When national security is not at stake, it is always better to have a full and frank debate than to rush to war. Extensive debate grounded in caution and insight could have uncovered important questions about the nature of the wars and the efficacy of committing the nation to war overseas. Certainly the men and women in uniform deserve the nation's best-considered judgment.

Furthermore, the panic-stricken Congress gave the president unusual authority to wage war in Vietnam and Iraq. Without a declaration of war, has Congress clearly spoken? It is much harder to get out of war than to get into it, and these two congressional resolutions paved the way for future problems. In both cases, some members of Congress have argued the White House deceived them. In both cases, some members of Congress are worried they indeed gave the president too much authority to wage war. And in both cases, it became increasingly difficult for Congress to register its objections to administration policy. The preferred time to debate the rationale for war is before troops are in the field. In both Iraq and Vietnam, Congress should have insisted on a more substantive debate before granting the president a war resolution. In Vietnam, Congress eventually rescinded the president's authority to wage war in its name. Will the

same be true in Iraq? Perhaps, but major differences in strategic doctrine and operations in Iraq may give the Bush administration more
time to convince Americans that the new war aim, building a stable
coalition government, is worth U.S. blood and treasure.

CHAPTER TWO

THE MILITARY HALF

I HAPPEN to know something about Vietnam," declared Senator John McCain in reaction to a Senate colleague who claimed Iraq and Vietnam were the same war. "It is a totally false comparison."[1] From a strategic and operational standpoint, McCain is unquestionably right. There are relatively few military similarities between the two wars. If the United States went to war in Iraq and Vietnam with the same high-minded idealism, heightened threat perceptions, and congressional support, it sent its soldiers to very different conflicts.

There are several important distinctions between the Iraq and Vietnam wars. For one, the size and scope of the conflicts are completely different. For another, Vietnam began as an insurgency, then escalated into a conventional war; in Iraq, the war started as a conventional invasion and then deteriorated into a guerrilla war. The insurgencies also share little in common, and the geopolitical climate has changed dramatically in the last thirty years. Furthermore, the armed forces the United States has sent into combat in each war have little in common. To reason by historical analogy requires making distinctions.

DIFFERENCES IN SIZE AND SCOPE OF THE WARS

One of the most significant differences between the Iraq and Vietnam wars is size and scope. In almost every conceivable way, the Vietnam War drew more of the nation's resources than has the war in Iraq. For example, U.S. troop levels in Vietnam peaked in April 1969 at 543,000.[2] American forces included nine U.S. Army and Marine Corps divisions plus several subdivisional combat units. Each year, over 100,000 U.S. troops served in the region as support staff for in-country personnel. In fact, more Americans served in Vietnam than in any other foreign war in U.S. history, with the exception of World War II. Another 100,000 troops fought in Vietnam each year from U.S. allies, especially South Korea, Thailand, Australia, New Zealand, and the Philippines.[3] Most important, the Republic of Vietnam Armed Forces (RVNAF), America's South Vietnamese allies, fielded over one million soldiers at the peak of the war.[4] The high-water mark for allied forces in the field was nearly 1.6 million troops.

Combined Communist forces of the People's Army of Vietnam (PAVN) and the People's Liberation Armed Forces (PLAF)—known in the West as the Vietcong—also numbered well over one million soldiers under arms.[5] If the PLAF's irregular guerrillas and political cadres who carried out strategic violence are added to the total, Communist troop levels overall approach those of the United States and its allies. In addition, the 200,000 Chinese combat engineers who served in North Vietnam released PAVN main-force infantry units to the southern battlefield.[6] Soviet advisers were also plentiful in the early years of the war, but their numbers declined substantially after the introduction of U.S. ground troops in March 1965. Hanoi had no problem drawing on its reserves, and it likely could have mobilized nearly 1.5 million soldiers for the final push against Saigon had that been necessary. A compulsory draft law passed in 1958 assured PAVN generals of adequate manpower to meet their force-level requirements for as long as the Americans remained in Vietnam. Military planners connected to the North's political bureau constantly talked of a twenty-year protracted war.[7]

The 3.2 million total combatants available each year in the theater of operations in Vietnam dwarf the troop levels in Iraq on all sides. U.S. troops fighting in Iraq have never totaled more than 150,000, and it is unlikely that Congress will allow that number to rise significantly. The most reliable figures put the insurgency—in all its various forms—at roughly 20,000.[8] As a meaningful measure, therefore, the total number of allied troops and insurgents fighting in Iraq today equals no more than 5 percent of those who annually fought in Vietnam. Still, some evidence suggests that the U.S. presence in Iraq is causing an increase in the number of enemy combatants. The number of external forces fighting in Iraq is also difficult to measure, but most U.S. intelligence analysts agree it does not approach the 200,000 Chinese combat engineers who found their way to Vietnam.[9] Furthermore, even if there is significant external support for the insurgency in Iraq, no nonstate actors can bring the resources to bear on the battlefield that Vietnam's two allies—the Soviet Union and China—did throughout the 1960s.

The Vietnam War, unlike the war in Iraq, also had a huge and sustained air component. From 1960 until the 1973 Paris peace accords, the United States dropped 8 million tons of bombs on the Indochina theater.[10] That quantity represents some of the most intense bombing in history. By comparison, in all of World War II, British and U.S. bomber forces dropped a relatively small 1.2 million tons of bombs in all of Europe.[11] In Iraq, the initial limited air campaign has given way to a "clear and hold" strategy on the ground. The Bush administration does seem to have learned one valuable lesson from Vietnam: It is difficult to accomplish political objectives with high-level strategic bombing. Ironically, the Johnson and Nixon administrations could have learned the same lesson if they had only listened to the intelligence community and the civilians in the Defense Department who had studied the matter thoroughly.

During the Vietnam War, a number of comprehensive studies were made to measure the effectiveness of the bombing campaign against North Vietnam. Drawing in part on the metrics used in the strategic bombing studies of World War II, the Defense Department examined the impact of the bombing on enemy morale, recruitment for the armed services, military production, and infiltration rates. In 1966 and 1967, a group of leading scientists under the auspices of the JASON Division of the Institute for Defense Analyses decided that U.S. bombing had not produced the desired result. The 1967 JASON study concluded that "as of October 1967, the U.S. bombing of North Vietnam has had no measurable effect on Hanoi's ability to mount and support military operations in the South." Furthermore, the report stressed that the bombing had not even achieved the limited goal of reducing the flow of men and supplies from North to South along the Ho Chi Minh Trail. In an unqualified dismissal of claims of the air-power enthusiasts, the study concluded:

> Since the beginning of Rolling Thunder, the air strikes on NVN, the flow of men and material from NVN to SVN has greatly

increased, and present evidence provides no basis for concluding that the damage inflicted on North Vietnam by the bombing program has had any significant effect on this flow. In short, the flow of men and material from North Vietnam to the South appears to reflect Hanoi's intentions rather than capabilities even in the face of the bombing.[12]

Key officials at the State Department and the Central Intelligence Agency's own studies confirmed the JASON findings. Despite this pessimistic reporting, the Joint Chiefs of Staff and U.S. military commanders in Vietnam declared the bombing had succeeded. Many policymakers and military leaders still believe this today. They argue that more bombing, not less, was needed to turn the tide in Vietnam.

Some military leaders with Vietnam experience doubt these claims, however, and they have had substantial influence on the Bush administration's military policies in Iraq. Generals Colin Powell and Norman Schwarzkopf, both Vietnam veterans, argued during the first Gulf War that air power is useful only in limited circumstances. In the planning leading up to that war, Powell and Schwarzkopf told the elder President Bush that the secondary plan for attacking Iraq in order to oust the Iraqi army from Kuwait was dependent upon coordinated attacks on land, sea, and air. The president asked, "Now Colin, you and Norm are really sure that air power alone can't do it?" Powell responded, "Mr. President, I wish to God that I could assure you that air power alone could do it but you can't take that chance. We've gotta take the initiative out of the enemy's hands if we're going to go to war. We've got to make sure that [this is] . . . there is no ordained conclusion and outcome, that there'll be no second guessing . . . that we will be successful with this plan and this is the plan we recommend."[13] Military planners for the Iraq War have repeatedly testified the first Gulf War taught them many lessons for how to attack Iraq.[14] After the initial invasion in March 2003, U.S. military planners convinced the younger President Bush the war was a ground war. It is unlikely, therefore, the nation will mount a bombing campaign in Iraq that mirrors that used in Vietnam. The United States does rely on an airmobile strategy in Iraq, but the purpose is primarily to avoid deadly truck convoys.

The Bush administration has also been careful not to use air power to strike at insurgents in large civilian population centers. Although there have been a significant number of civilian deaths in Iraq, U.S. military commanders remind their tactical planners that bombing civilian targets in Vietnam was one of the antiwar movement's major weapons against the Johnson and Nixon administrations. Over one million Vietnamese civilians died in South Vietnam.[15] Given that the Iraqi insurgents have no air force and only limited air defenses, it would be a tragic mistake if the Bush administration did return to a Vietnam-style air war.

U.S. military planners in Iraq are unlikely to increase the size and scope of the air war in part because they do not want a repeat of the number of casualties—civilian and military—that massive firepower produced in Vietnam. Hanoi recently announced that 3.2 million Communist troops and civilians were killed during the war.[16] This huge number, when combined with RVNAF losses, represents over 10 percent of the entire population of Vietnam. That would be the equivalent today of losing to war 30 million Americans, or the entire populations of New York City, Los Angeles, Chicago, and Boston combined. Add to the Vietnam toll the number of Laotians and

Cambodian Khmer lost, and Vietnam becomes one of the deadliest wars in modern history.

The United States also suffered heavy losses in the Vietnam War. Over 58,000 U.S. servicemen were killed and another 150,000 were wounded.[17] The RVNAF lost over 250,000 troops.[18] These losses made it difficult for U.S. policymakers to stay the course in Vietnam, especially when Congress and large segments of the American people began to question the rationale for the war. Maintaining credibility around the globe and ensuring an independent—if not democratic—South Vietnam did not seem worth all the death and destruction. The military used massive firepower to break Hanoi's will to continue the fight, but most policy analysts today suggest the air war in Vietnam might have only strengthened the morale of North Vietnam and its citizens.[19] In South Vietnam, the air war certainly turned many friends into foes. Those in the military today with Vietnam experience caution the Bush administration against high-level strategic bombing and an air campaign that wreaked havoc on a country whose population was not much bigger than Iraq's is today.

So far, it does not appear casualty figures in Iraq will approach those of Vietnam. As of February 2006, the death toll for young men and women in the U.S. armed services was 2,300. In January 2006, President Bush announced Iraq's civilian death toll was 35,000, although some estimates placed that number at closer to 100,000.[20] U.S. combat troops have been in Iraq since March 2003. In the comparable period in Vietnam, 1965–1967, there were 17,754 American casualties.[21] In the Iraq conflict, advances in medical technology and improved evacuation procedures have no doubt saved lives on both sides. Again, however, the size and scope of the Iraq and Vietnam wars account for the very different casualty projections. In all likelihood, the limited nature of the war in Iraq will continue to keep combat and civilian deaths from approaching Vietnam-level numbers. Still, casualties in Iraq are the highest in any U.S.-led war since Vietnam.

MILITARY OPERATIONS IN VIETNAM

On the surface, military operations in Iraq also differ greatly from those in Vietnam, where most military operations took place in remote villages or jungle areas far from urban centers. Light-infantry battles with PAVN and PLAF troops dominated the military engagements. In Iraq, in sharp contrast, the war has had a distinctly urban flavor. Insurgents take cabs to their target areas and escape the same way. Leaders of the insurgency spend most of their days driving to remote areas of Iraq, just ahead of U.S. forces in armored personnel carriers. The car bomb has come to symbolize the war in Iraq largely because the road is the war's most significant center of gravity.[22] This situation, however, could lead the Bush administration to follow many of the same operational mistakes made in Vietnam. The focus there of most military operations was to kill insurgents; the focus in Iraq is the same. Night goggles and infrared sensors mean U.S. troops own the Iraqi night, and they use this advantage to strike at the heart of the insurgency. In the daytime, U.S. soldiers join their coalition allies in armored convoys to locate insurgent bases and destroy them.

As in Vietnam, however, the focus on killing insurgents carries risk. Historically, most successful counterinsurgency programs have concentrated on securing the civilian population and winning its public support. This battle for the hearts and minds of Iraqis need not follow the Vietnam pattern, which in the early to mid-1960s overly emphasized military objectives. In Iraq, U.S. forces are being forced off the streets and into their military vehicles, away from the very people they are supposed to be protecting. Moving toward a more mechanized response to the Iraqi insurgents plays into their hands because they hope that in the long battle against the new government in Baghdad, the United States will lose support among the Iraqi people. Thus, the insurgents will continue to create a threat environment that forces U.S. troops away from street patrols and light-infantry maneuvers. In asymmetrical wars, insurgents depend on the larger power to retreat from political objectives. This was certainly the case in Vietnam.

During the Kennedy years, the president employed a counterinsurgency formula designed to separate the fish from the water.[23] The "fish" were Communist guerrillas operating in the villages and hamlets of Vietnam. The "water" was the people of the rural areas in Vietnam, the bulk of the population. Military operations took the form of localized maneuvers to uproot insurgents and create pacified villages through the Strategic Hamlet Program. Kennedy's strategy met with only limited success, however, and the insurgency against Ngo Dinh Diem grew at an alarming rate. In trying to isolate the insurgents, U.S. and South Vietnamese troops precipitated an increase in their ranks. The violence in the countryside was too indiscriminate to keep neutral villagers out of the fray. Another major problem was that Diem had very little interest in the political war in the villages of South Vietnam, and the Americans were so culturally removed from Vietnamese politics that their nation-building efforts fell far short of the desired goal. It was clear by 1963 Kennedy had to find a strategy that promised more success in the political war against the National Liberation Front (NLF). At the time of his assassination in November 1963, he was exploring his strategic options.

When Lyndon Johnson assumed the presidency following Kennedy's assassination, his inherited advisers told him that continuing along the same path in Vietnam promised few satisfactory results.[24] The president either had to get in more forcefully or get out, but the current strategy was a recipe for disaster. Ultimately, Johnson chose war. In slow and incremental steps, the president took the nation to war because he saw no other viable options. Though Johnson and his key advisers were pessimistic at times about the chances of success in Vietnam, they saw no alternative but to increase the military pressure against Hanoi. Johnson rejected the thinking of several experts who claimed the only way to win in Vietnam was to keep military action limited and increase the political activity in Vietnam's villages.[25] After Ho rejected Johnson's calls for a Mekong River project, the president focused more forcefully on the military half of the war, what he called the war "in cold blood."[26] Johnson eventually approved the introduction of U.S. combat troops in March 1965 coupled with the sustained bombing of North Vietnam, known as Operation Rolling Thunder.

Strategically, the United States fought a protracted war during the Johnson years (1964–1969) designed to inflict intolerable casualties on Communist forces through the use of massive U.S. firepower. Believing the war had mutated from a guerrilla conflict to large-unit warfare by 1965—and thus had shifted from the political to the military struggle—U.S. military planners hoped to crush the PAVN and the PLAF, forcing Hanoi to sue for peace. The goal was to reach the "crossover" or "breaking point" when the casualties simply became too much for the Vietnamese to accept.[27] This strategy was the brainchild of General William C. Westmoreland, whom Johnson had sent to Vietnam in 1964 as the commander of MACV (Military Assistance Command—Vietnam), which was responsible for all allied military operations in Vietnam.

There was some simple calculus involved in Westmoreland's strategy that kept U.S. military operations in line with Johnson's political and foreign policy needs. Westmoreland asked two straightforward questions: How many U.S. troops would it take to inflict significant enough casualties on the enemy that Hanoi would be forced to surrender? And, how long would it take? According to Westmoreland, it would take hundreds of thousands of U.S. troops and years, not months, to reach the crossover point.[28] He hoped the mission could be accomplished in a shorter time through employment of the other elements of grand strategy—economic and political considerations—but he was prepared to see the war of attrition through to the end.

At the heart of Westmoreland's strategy was the "search and destroy" mission. Waging what he called the "most sophisticated war in history," Westmoreland ordered U.S. troops to locate and eliminate PLAF and PAVN main-infantry forces throughout South Vietnam. According to the general, "They had to be pounded with artillery and bombs and eventually brought to battle on the ground if they were not forever to remain a threat."[29] Once U.S. forces destroyed these regular units, the RVNAF could take over pacifying the guerrilla movement in the hamlets and villages of South Vietnam. Westmoreland used air power to support forces in battle according to what some scholars have called the "pile-on concept," in which U.S. troops encircled enemy units and called in the bombing raids.[30] Entire areas of South Vietnam were designated as "free-fire zones," which could be attacked without regard for anyone caught in the line of fire.

The problem with Westmoreland's strategy was twofold: First, Hanoi matched each U.S. escalation of the war; second, the Communists had conditioned their people to accept unusually high losses in the battle for independence and unification. PAVN infiltration into South Vietnam was crucial for victory and was completely dependent on the now-infamous Ho Chi Minh Trail. What was initially a makeshift footpath running through eastern Laos and Cambodia to South Vietnam was transformed into a major transportation system that required hundreds of thousands of combat engineers to maintain.[31] There was also a little-known sea version of the trail that brought men and supplies to the Cau Mau peninsula in South Vietnam.[32] Despite heavy bombing and sophisticated land mines, the United States had little impact on the flow of men and supplies from North to South. According to one Communist Party leader, the Ho Chi Minh Trail was "the lifeline of the revolution."[33] During peak times of the war, Hanoi could move over 400 tons of supplies down the trail each week and as many as 5,000 soldiers per month.[34]

Although the war reached a military stalemate in 1967, it was clear to President Johnson following the 1968 Tet offensive that Westmoreland's protracted-war strategy was no longer viable. Despite enormous hardships and mounting casualties, the Communists continued to replenish their troops. The promised breaking point seemed no closer in 1968 than it had in 1965, despite the huge sacrifice in American lives and funds. Much of South Vietnam had been laid waste through U.S. bombing missions and search-and-destroy operations. Yet there was little to show for all the death and destruction. Each American blow "was like a sledgehammer on a floating cork," reported journalist Malcom Browne, who covered the war.[35] Accordingly, Johnson relieved Westmoreland of his command in June 1968, replacing him with General Creighton Abrams.

Almost immediately, Abrams altered U.S. military strategy in Vietnam. Instead of relying on search-and-destroy missions that supported a protracted-war strategy, Abrams introduced the concept of pacification and a "clear and hold" strategy. Coupled with increased air attacks against North Vietnam, pacification and "clear and hold" promised to rid South Vietnam of its most important source of agitation, the PLAF and the NLF's political infrastructure. In short, pacification was a multifaceted program that combined incentives for NLF cadres to defect to the government's side along with targeted arrests and assassinations of the front's political leaders. In addition, U.S. troops and their RVNAF allies focused military operations on key areas in South Vietnam instead of roaming the countryside searching for Communist troops. The idea was to secure villagers in South Vietnam and, at the same time, to make strategic military strikes against the Communists. By 1970 pacification seemed to be a success. The South Vietnamese government controlled more territory than it had at any time since 1961, and NLF ranks had been seriously damaged.[36]

In a 2005 essay in *Foreign Affairs*, Melvin Laird, President Nixon's former secretary of defense, argued that pacification worked well in Vietnam and should be used in Iraq. In his view, the NLF was "largely suppressed by a combination of persuasion and force."[37] Furthermore, the success of pacification turned the tide of the war in favor of South Vietnam. At the time of the complete U.S. withdrawal in January 1973, Laird believed the Nixon administration had left a healthy Saigon to defend itself against the Communists. Pacification had changed the balance of forces in South Vietnam, and victory was all but certain. Only Soviet interference and congressional budget cuts kept this reality from happening. Whereas Moscow was sending Hanoi more than $1 billion, the U.S. Congress cut all funding to South Vietnam. According to Laird, without U.S. funding, "South Vietnam was quickly overrun."[38] Congress took away all that pacification had gained.

Pacification has had its critics, though, and several Vietnam War experts have disputed those who claim the war was won on the ground and then lost in Washington. David Elliott, a professor at Pomona College who spent five years in Vietnam with the U.S. Army and the Rand Corporation during the war, has concluded that optimistic reports about pacification's success are "wrong."[39] William Turley, author of the influential text *The Second Indochina War*, told a *Boston Globe* reporter "he cannot understand why anyone would think 'clear and hold' was a success in Vietnam."[40] According to Arnold Isaacs, who covered the last three years of the Vietnam War for the *Baltimore Sun*, pacification was not the resounding success Laird has claimed it was. Isaacs noted, "A war may be going well but it isn't won if the enemy is still fighting, much less if the bloodiest battles are still to come, as Vietnam's were. And it most certainly isn't won if, when the fighting stops, the flag over the battleground—in this case, the entire country of Vietnam—is the enemy's."[41]

Pacification was considerably successful against the PLAF, and evidence suggests that South Vietnam controlled more territory in 1970 than it had previously. Complicating this issue, however, was the fact that many hamlets listed as "secure" simply had been emptied as part of the U.S. program of forced draft urbanization. Thousands of peasants had to flee to South Vietnam's cities because of the destruction of their local environments. Some U.S. analysts believed that forcing people to the cities would give the South Vietnamese government greater control over the population.[42] The thinking in Washington was that because Saigon could not effectively mobilize the rural Vietnamese, making them dependent would eliminate the need for massive political organization. Emptying the countryside fit Saigon's needs, but it also may have given a false reading on the security of South Vietnam's hamlets.

Other problems with the data also contradict the premise of pacification as a success. There have been questions about the reliability of the surveys used to determine whether the strategy of pacification was working. The basic metric used for evaluation was the Hamlet Evaluation Survey (HES), which counted the number of Communists "eliminated" or "rallied" (those who joined the government) and the number of villages under South Vietnamese control. According to HES surveys, the Saigon government controlled more villages in 1971 than it had at any other time since the 1968 Tet offensive. Some officials familiar with HES data, however, have said HES reports commonly were inflated.[43] They also have explained that forced draft urbanization made it difficult to examine villages. Furthermore, by 1971, the problem in South Vietnam was the increased presence of PAVN main-force infantry units. Pacification may have been a success against the PLAF, but it now seems clear that whatever losses the PAVN suffered could be replaced.

There is some merit, however, to the argument advanced by Lewis Sorley, a former U.S. Army officer with Vietnam experience who also holds a Ph.D. from Johns Hopkins University. In his book *A Better War*, Sorley examined Abrams's policies and concluded that pacification was indeed making inroads in Vietnam, but that policymakers in Washington snatched defeat from the jaws of victory.[44] Sorley correctly analyzed that regardless of what was happening on the ground, the Nixon administration and the Congress were committed to a U.S. withdrawal. Beginning in February 1970, it was official U.S. policy not to enforce a mutual withdrawal from South Vietnam.[45] PAVN troops—ten main-force infantry divisions, it turned out—were allowed to stay in South Vietnam following a U.S. unilateral troop withdrawal, because it was the only way the Nixon administration could negotiate an end to the war. Feeling domestic political pressure for that objective, the Nixon administration was negotiating in Paris a position that Sorley and many others have claimed was counter to the military reality on the ground. For Laird, Congress compounded the problem when it cut off funding for South Vietnam.

The debate over pacification likely will rage for years. Interestingly, there are reports that many current Bush administration officials have read Sorley's book and expressed support for the ideas contained in Laird's essay.[46] Some White House voices support a pacification strategy in Iraq, and more than one Bush administration official has used the words "clear and hold." It will be interesting if the Bush team does revisit the Vietnam War for a strategy in Iraq. The critics of such a move are many, and there is no doubt that if the United States does launch an accelerated pacification program in Iraq, the debate will grow more intense.

KILLING INSURGENTS: THE STRATEGY IN IRAQ

Notwithstanding the controversy over pacification, Laird was correct to point out that Iraq's conventional forces have already been defeated, so that the "insurgency is the only enemy."[47] The problem will remain the battle for the hearts and minds of the Iraqis. Despite Laird's desire to see Abrams's strategy used in Iraq, military operations there have begun to resemble those used by Westmoreland in Vietnam. U.S. forces in Iraq have adopted an attrition strategy. American troops conduct numerous raids into hostile areas, hoping to arrest insurgents and gain intelligence to cripple the antigovernment movement. The idea is to kill as many insurgents as possible and at the same time provide security to the Iraqi people. But, as in Vietnam, this is a difficult balance to strike. As car bombings increase, it becomes more difficult for U.S. forces to focus on the political war. If the road is the center of gravity in the war thus far, it is up to the U.S. command to figure out a way to reestablish contact with the Iraqi people. The Bush administration sees the development of the Iraqi security forces as a key component to its political and military strategy, and there is no doubt that this is the direction the war must take. President Bush is fond of saying, "Our strategy can be summed up this way: As the Iraqis stand up, we will stand down." Critics of this policy, such as Andrew Krepenevich, an expert on the army in Vietnam, argue the president is describing a withdrawal plan, not a political and military strategy.[48] Clearly, the main military objective in Iraq is to put down the insurgency, even if there is not a specific strategy to accomplish that goal. It would be a mistake, however, for the Bush team to look to Vietnam for a strategy against insurgents in Iraq and to ignore the political war.

Whether the Bush administration can keep the war limited and focus more on the security of the Iraqi people will depend in large part on its reading of the insurgency in Iraq. If the insurgency continues to grow, will the United States need more troops? Will U.S.

military planners advocate a more aggressive military strategy? In the absence of success against the insurgents, will the United States resort to a deadly air war? Will the American people lose faith in the war if U.S. casualties mount at the hands of the insurgents? Many of these questions revolve around the character of the insurgency and the nature of its relationship to other militant groups in the region. Although little is known about the insurgency in Iraq today, there are some fundamental differences between it and Vietnam's National Liberation Front.

THE NATIONAL LIBERATION FRONT

The NLF was completely homegrown and possessed a very specific—and easily recognizable—military and political agenda. Born in December 1960 in the mangrove swamps of Tay Ninh province, near Vietnam's border with Cambodia, the NLF, derogatorily known in the West as the Vietcong, was a classical Communist front organization. After six years of trying to liberate South Vietnam through political means alone, the Vietnamese Communist Party finally decided the time had come to overthrow Ngo Dinh Diem, South Vietnam's first president, by force. To accomplish this goal, the party approved the formation of a broad-based united front "to rally all patriotic classes and sections of the people . . . to oppose the U.S.-Diem regime."[49] The NLF was under direct control of the party's central committee but worked tirelessly to recruit non-Communists to its cause. Political cadres were active in urban areas, Diem's only base of support, and, of course, the NLF was interested in winning over the rural areas.

In the early years of the war, the NLF's insurgency relied on a combination of political and military maneuvers to enlist cadres. Its goals, as stated in a captured party document, were to "lessen enemy pressure, oppose military operations and terrorism, oppose the strategic hamlet program, and halt the seizure of land and the corvée labor system [conscripted unpaid workers]."[50] To accomplish these objectives, the NLF engaged in a people's war in villages throughout South Vietnam. A concept borrowed in part from the Chinese Communists, "people's war" stressed the political nature of the military struggle.

In practice, people's war relied heavily on the NLF cadres' ability to communicate the ideas of the revolution to a war-ravaged rural population in South Vietnam. According to one of the most important party publications on the village war, "Needs of the Revolution," NLF cadres should "choose the right moment to act . . . when the people's rights have been endangered." The NLF political leadership defined these threats as "corruption, high taxation, forced money donations, land robbing, military draft." After these conditions were identified, party leaders explained, "struggle movements can then be launched in favor of freedom of travel, freedom to work, freedom of trade, freedom to move to a new part of the country, and for village council elections."[51] Cadres used this technique to convince villagers they were the vanguard of a new social movement that would return control of their hamlets to them. Using this political message, NLF cadre ranks swelled by nearly 300 percent a month during its first year.[52]

Of course, there was a military side to the insurgency as well. In the early years of the NLF, the insurgency used terror to send a message to Diem and his supporters that they could no longer have their way in South Vietnam.[53] Car bombs, convoy ambushes, night raids on villages, and political assassinations were common insurgent activities. By late 1961, however, the insurgency was regularized in the sense that the NLF formed several main-force infantry divisions that received significant material and technical support from Hanoi. Although the concept of people's war remained in place, insurgents now practiced more conventional forms of warfare. Nowhere was this shift more apparent than at the battle of Ap Bac in January 1963 when the PLAF's 261st Main-Force Battalion shot down five U.S. helicopters and killed 60 RVNAF soldiers while suffering only minor losses.[54]

In the early years of the war, President Kennedy feared the growing insurgency in Vietnam as much as any cold-war problem. To deal with the NLF, he quickly developed counterinsurgency measures in Vietnam based on the British experience in Malaya.[55] Instead of sending in U.S. combat troops, Kennedy created strategic hamlets, designed to isolate the NLF from the peasants by building new protected hamlets. U.S. advisers relocated villagers to these newly constructed safe havens to separate them from the Communists and facilitate South Vietnam's social programs. The goal, according to counterinsurgency expert Roger Hilsman, was to reduce NLF cadres to "hungry, marauding bands of outlaws devoting all their energies to remaining alive."[56] Of course, the United States and its South Vietnamese allies experienced little success against the insurgency in the early years of the war. Only after the battles became more conventional, and the insurgency gave way to coordinated attacks with North Vietnam's People's Army, did the United States experience any military success.

The NLF's relationship to the Communists in Hanoi was complex and at times strained. Although the NLF was a classical Communist front, there were regional differences within Vietnam's Communist Party. During the early years of the war, 1955–1960, northern members of the Party did not want to launch all-out military attacks against Diem and South Vietnam.[57] Instead, they had hoped to regroup from heavy losses suffered in the war that had just ended with the French and to reunite Vietnam through political means alone. Some northerners even held out promise that the elections called for in the 1954 Geneva accords would take place, and that Ho Chi Minh, president of Vietnam's Communist Party, would take his rightful place as the leader of a united Vietnam. Political leaders in Hanoi were also careful to follow the wishes of their allies in Moscow and Beijing. Both China and the Soviet Union supported the political struggle against "imperialism" in Vietnam in the mid-to-late 1950s, fearing the United States might once again intervene in the region if Ho Chi Minh launched a military struggle against his rivals inside Vietnam. Still smarting from the Korean War, neither socialist superpower wanted to provoke the United States into any action that might threaten the regional balance of power.

Southerners believed their northern counterparts should support a more vigorous armed struggle against Diem, no matter what Hanoi's benefactors wanted. They constantly pushed for a more active military stance in South Vietnam and even launched insurgent attacks against Diem's forces in 1959 without Hanoi's approval. Ultimately, party leaders in Hanoi had to approve military action or risk losing control of the insurgency in South Vietnam.[58] The creation of the NLF, therefore, was a way for the party to gain more influence over the insurgency and its political and military operations. U.S. intelligence officers stationed in Vietnam recognized the relationship between Hanoi and the NLF soon after the NLF's formation, but they had a difficult job convincing Washington that the insurgency was not a cross-border invasion.

From the earliest days of the Vietnam War, key members of the Kennedy administration claimed Saigon was under attack from Communist forces originating in North Vietnam. The United States supported this claim with several White House position papers concluding that Communist North Vietnam was trying to take an independent and democratic South Vietnam by force.[59] Washington also developed doctrine to reflect that perception. U.S. military officials first assigned to Vietnam believed any attack against South Vietnam would come from the North. The thinking among American leaders in Washington and Saigon reflected previous U.S. combat experience in Korea. The general outlook of U.S. Army doctrine was that revolution could not be instigated or successful without the support of an external sponsoring power.[60] Experience in Korea suggested the guerrillas operating freely in South Vietnam were the early warning of cross-border conventional attacks, far more serious than any local insurgency.[61]

U.S. officials now know, however, that the NLF insurgency was composed exclusively of southerners. In fact, even after the NLF's formation in 1960, Hanoi was reluctant to send main-force infantry units south to support the insurgency. Only at the Communist Party's ninth plenum in December 1963 did the political bureau agree to aid the southern revolution with arms and men.[62] Following that decision, it took nearly two years for these approved troops and supplies to make their way south down the Ho Chi Minh Trail. These troops arrived just in time for the now-infamous battle of the Ia Drang Valley.

One key difference between the NLF and the insurgency in Iraq is that the front in Vietnam was always a public fixture. The NLF's Foreign Relations Commission routinely published position papers and met with foreigners in Vietnam, Europe, Canada, and even the United States.[63] Leaders of the Vietnamese insurgency were symbols of the modern revolution, and it was easy to ascertain (if not support) their program. Eventually, key members of the Vietnamese insurgency sat with Americans in Paris to hammer out the details of the final peace accord. The war had always been about the political future of Vietnam below the seventeenth parallel, and the insurgency was at the forefront of that discussion every step of the way. U.S. intelligence experts in Saigon easily figured out who led the insurgency and what their goals where. They simply had to pick up the local newspaper or turn on the radio. There were no complicating factors of nationality, ethnicity, tribe, religion, or ideology. The NLF's message and goals were clear to anyone who cared enough to find out. The insurgency supported the forced withdrawal of all U.S. troops, the overthrow of the Saigon regime, and the unification of Vietnam under the socialist banner.

Furthermore, Ho Chi Minh was such a powerful public symbol that he clearly represented the revolution to the international community. Throughout the war, Ho's image and words were an important propaganda tool not only for the Communist Party but also for those who opposed U.S. intervention. He rallied supporters to the revolutionary cause during his life, and in death became perhaps an even more significant international symbol. It was not uncommon at antiwar rallies worldwide to see images of Ho or the Vietnamese flag. At the height of the protests at the 1968 Democratic National Convention in Chicago, antiwar activists waved the NLF flag high atop statues in Grant Park. A familiar chant at the marches on Washington was "Ho, Ho, Ho Chi Minh; the NLF is going to win." Throughout the war, the revolutionary movement in Vietnam presented easily recognizable platforms and symbols of national identity.

WHO LEADS THE INSURGENCY IN IRAQ?

In Iraq today the insurgents and their goals remain a mystery. By most accounts, the major insurgency groups in Iraq are (1) the Supreme Council for the Islamic Revolution in Iraq (al-Majlis al-A'la lil-Thawara al-Islamiyya fil-'Iraq), a Shia nationalist group headed by Abdel 'Aziz al-Hakim; (2) the Shiite resistance movement headed by Moqtada al-Sadr, one of the most adamant opponents of the U.S. occupation of Iraq; (3) a small Salafi group based in Fallujah headed by Umar Husayn Hadid; (4) a Sunni group called the "Iraqi Islamic Army"; (5) former Baathists connected to Saddam's regime; and (6) foreign jihadist groups working with Osama bin Laden's ally Abu Musab al-Zarqawi, such as Ansar al-Islam. All these groups oppose the U.S. presence in Iraq, but it is difficult to gauge their interests beyond desire for a U.S. withdrawal.

Some insurgent groups, including the Supreme Council for the Islamic Revolution, support pan-Arab nationalism. The radical Shiites connected to Moqtada al-Sadr seek a theocracy in Iraq along with a U.S. withdrawal. They cling to the idea of a Taliban-like Islamic government coming to power and promoting Islamic revolution throughout the region. Taken together, the various insurgent groups seem focused more on toppling the existing Iraqi government and embarrassing the United States than on offering a clear political alternative. What the insurgents oppose is clear, but what they support is not. The insurgents in Iraq do not have a carefully translated ten-point program of the sort the National Liberation Front did in Vietnam.[64]

At this point, violence seems to be the only unifying factor in the Iraqi insurgency. For the core of Sunni insurgents, any individual, group, or organization willing to use violence against the occupation is seen as a potential ally. Direct action against the Americans and their Baghdad allies is the focus of all political and military activity. In late December 2005, however, there were signs that the insurgency was turning on itself. Reports that al-Qaeda fighters were the target of Iraqi insurgent strikes suggest that anti-Americanism might not be enough to unite the disparate groups in Iraq. Still, it is quite possible trained jihadists can gain control of the insurgency inside Iraq and turn it into another Afghanistan—where the government has nominal control of the population—once U.S. troops are forced to withdraw. One favored tactic of the insurgents is to attack civilian populations nominally under U.S. control. This violence is designed not only to increase U.S. casualties but also to show ordinary Iraqis their allies cannot protect them. The overall goal is to force the United States to leave Iraq before the new government can solidify its control of the country. Undermining Iraqis' confidence in the United States is the cornerstone of that program.

Although this tactic has met with some initial success, the Iraqi insurgency still lacks a unifying agenda other than pan-Arabism and anti-Americanism. No single leader or organization has galvanized the opposition parties in Iraq, and it is unlikely an Iraqi counterpart of Ho Chi Minh will step forward to represent the insurgents' political goals. The only discernible endgame for the insurgents is their angry reaction to events in Iraq. Without the national leadership projected by a charismatic figure, the insurgents ultimately will begin to alienate the population with their indiscriminate attacks on civilian targets. All the cold war's most radical leaders had a political agenda that fueled their revolutionary ideology. The world knew what Mao, Che, Fidel, and Ho stood for in the cold war and knew how they hoped to accomplish their political goals. In Iraq, the insurgents lack any proactive political agenda. Should the insurgents achieve their limited objectives of a U.S. withdrawal and an end to the current government in Baghdad, the movement probably would turn on itself.

Some supporters of the Iraqi insurgency have declared it premature for one group to dominate the political direction of the anti-American movement. They argue that the Iraqi insurgency is much like China's united front strategy in the 1930s or Vietnam's NLF during the 1960s.[65] This is a serious misreading of history. The united front in Asian Communist movements always made temporary alliances with potential enemies as long as they supported the revolution's overall goals, but at no time did the party relinquish control of the insurgency or its political and military movements. In China and Vietnam, the revolution's main objective was to replace one social system with another. The party offered a clear political alternative to the government in power. In Iraq, the various insurgent groups have not followed the same path. This is not a people's war. Its only unifying theme seems to be the old Bolshevik adage "the worse, the better."

Despite the lack of unifying message or national political ideology delivered by a charismatic leader, the Iraqi insurgency continues to present the United States with a number of difficult problems. Increasing attacks on civilian targets have prompted U.S. military commanders in Iraq to launch more anti-insurgent patrols. This gives U.S. forces a target, but it also reinforces the notion that the United States is an occupying force. Much as the British in Ireland during "the troubles" of the 1960s and 1970s, the United States finds itself patrolling vast stretches of Iraq behind heavy armor. U.S. patrols have focused on many areas in the Red Zone—the generally unsecured provinces of Anbar, Nineveh, and Salah ad Din—to strike at the heart of the insurgency. Missions in the Red Zone have left the Green Zone—the heavily fortified area around Baghdad—open to insurgent attacks. The insurgents understand that attacks against civilians in the Green Zone shake the confidence of ordinary Iraqis.

The United States failed to win the hearts and minds of the peasants in Vietnam, and that same problem remains a significant obstacle to U.S. success in Iraq. A senior U.S. Army commander in Baghdad reported in 2004 that he did not view winning hearts and minds in Iraq as "one of the metrics of success."[66] If that attitude prevails, there could be a repeat of Vietnam. The political war is vital to success in Iraq, however defined. It is clear the government in Baghdad will not be a perfect democracy and the United States cannot solve all political problems among Iraq's rival political, ethnic, and religious groups. Still, by focusing on the political war instead of the Romanesque strategy of destroying all the insurgents, the Bush administration has a chance to rescue victory from defeat. Following the invasion of Iraq, many U.S. officials felt the United States had to "fix" Iraq because Americans had "broken it."[67] It may be true that the United States has a moral obligation not to abandon a country that was purposefully thrown into chaos, but it is also true that America must make prudent decisions in the political war. The insurgency is only part of the problem in Iraq. As was true in Vietnam, winning support of the population is more important to the long-term success of the government than killing insurgents.

AMERICAN TROOPS: TODAY AND YESTERDAY

Success in the political war in Iraq will require U.S. military commanders to rethink their mission. During the Vietnam War, such reflection was difficult. Today, however, the nature of the armed forces allows for more flexibility in strategic and operational thinking. There are vast differences between the U.S. troops sent to Vietnam and those sent to Iraq, and these distinctions may have an impact on the conduct and the outcome of the war. Differences in age, socioeconomic background, and education underscore the major changes that have occurred in the U.S. military in the past thirty years. Many of these differences stem from change in the selection of the armed forces. In the 1970s, the United States abandoned the military draft and moved to an all-volunteer army. The results have been dramatic.

During the Vietnam War, the selective service held a two-stage draft. In the first stage, young men were drafted by local draft boards following national guidelines and requirements. In 1970 the Nixon administration introduced a lottery system that ended many of the loopholes in the early draft. Draft calls mounted to 30,000 to 40,000 per month during peak times of the war.[68] The forces that fought in Vietnam, however, were drawn from the largest generation of young men in the nation's history. Although 27 million American males came of draft age from 1964 until the Paris peace accords in 1973, less than 10 percent of that total served in Vietnam.[69] According to most official accounts, working-class soldiers (those from families earning under $7,500 in 1968 dollars) made up 80 percent of the enlisted men.[70] An extensive study of Vietnam casualties from Illinois concluded that men from neighborhoods with median family incomes under $5,000 (in 1968 dollars) were four times more likely to die in combat in Vietnam than men from places with median family incomes above $15,000.[71] Another revealing statistic is that 80 percent of the enlisted men who served in Vietnam had no more than a high school education.[72] In short, Vietnam was a working-class war.

It was also a war that took America's youngest soldiers. During the Vietnam conflict, most of the volunteers and draftees were teenagers; the average age was nineteen.[73] In World War II, by contrast, the average American soldier was twenty-six years old.[74] The draft came at age eighteen, although young men could, with the consent of a guardian, enlist in the U.S. Marine Corps at age seventeen. In a war rich in ironies, one of the greatest was that most soldiers serving in Vietnam could go to war but not vote. This factor influenced the change to lower the voting age from twenty-one to eighteen by constitutional amendment in 1971. Some states where soldiers trained, especially in the rural South, also did not allow alcohol consumption for anyone under twenty-one years of age. An eighteen-year-old man could not drink and could not vote in the United States from 1965 until 1971, but he could be drafted to serve in Vietnam.

In 1973, however, the Nixon administration began to move away from forced conscription, partly to quiet its domestic critics. The thinking in Washington was that antiwar protests would die down if the draft were eliminated. Some military leaders also argued that an all-volunteer force would reduce some of the training and discipline problems encountered in Vietnam. The all-volunteer army came into being in 1973 when the induction authority of the Selective Service

Act of 1940 (with its amendments) expired. The Nixon administration realized the draft had created deep divisions in the country and had called the "unwilling" to serve.[75] In 1975 the Selective Service System entered what it called "deep standby posture." This meant that unless there was a national emergency, Congress would not authorize the resumption of inductions. Beginning in late 1979, Congress approved measures to increase military preparedness by mandating that all young men had to register within thirty days of their eighteenth birthday. By early 1980 the all-volunteer armed forces were firmly established.

Along with changes in the draft laws came increased professional-ization in the ranks. Today's soldiers in the all-volunteer armed forces have years of training at the individual and subunit level. Most soldiers who saw service in Vietnam served one twelve-month tour of active duty in-country. Their military service was limited in time and scope. Even though more career servicemen served in Vietnam than those who were drafted (only 25 percent of those who served in Vietnam were drafted), there was still a sense that the armed forces did not have years of experience in service. From 1960 until 1973, the average enlistee in the armed forces served two years.[76] In Iraq, in sharp contrast, the average soldier has had seven years of active-duty experience.[77] Furthermore, changes in training have given today's soldiers significantly more time working together in combined operations. Significant reforms at the Pentagon, including the 1986 Goldwater-Nichols Reorganization Act, gave the chairman of the Joint Chiefs of Staff centralized operational authority. Prior to this act, each service chief was responsible for the operations of his branch. Goldwater-Nichols allowed for joint operations through a central command, and this had an enormous impact on soldiers and soldiering. By combining operations, the U.S. armed forces could train for several contingencies and for greater periods of time.

Other important distinctions between today's soldiers and those who fought in Vietnam pertain to personal background. In sharp contrast to the Vietnam era, the average age of an active-duty member of the armed services in 2005 was 28.3.[78] For active-duty troops serving in Iraq, the average age is 22.[79] When reservists—who are serving in Iraq in record numbers—are added to the tally, the average age increases significantly. Further, unlike Vietnam, Iraq is not a working-class war. Soldiers serving in today's armed forces come from families that have a slightly higher median income than the national average ($44,500 versus $44,300). The number of troops who held a high school diploma or its equivalent in 2005 (96 percent) is also considerably higher than in the Vietnam War (79 percent). Racially, the professional army of today nearly mirrors the society it vows to protect. According to the Department of Defense, whites make up 67 percent of the armed services compared with 71 percent of the civilian workforce. African Americans have a slightly higher representation in the military than in the workforce (17 percent versus 11 percent). Hispanic soldiers represent 9 percent of the armed forces and 11 percent of the civilian workforce.[80] During the Vietnam War, people of color served in numbers greater than their representation in the population as a whole.

The demographic differences between troops who served in Vietnam and those who served in Iraq as well as greater professionalization may also account for changing public attitudes toward men and women in uniform. Many Americans did not approve of the long hair, the nonstandard uniform worn by soldiers in the field (such as peace symbols on helmets), the Black Power Movement inside the armed forces in Vietnam, and especially the reported atrocities such as at My Lai. The data also indicate that many Americans believed drug use was destroying the army and the mission.[81] The stories of returning soldiers being met at U.S. airports by angry antiwar protesters became legendary.

This lack of support for troops was not always present. During the Vietnam War, the public's attitude toward U.S. troops shifted dramatically. In the early years of the war, when Kennedy sent U.S. advisers to Vietnam to help train RVNAF forces and tutor Ngo Dinh Diem, there was considerable support for the war and the troops. As the face of the war changed, and Lyndon Johnson introduced combat troops in March 1965 and gave them offensive military operations that summer, public support for the war began to wane. By 1967 a majority of Americans opposed U.S. intervention.[82] Particularly noteworthy for this discussion, however, is that American attitudes toward U.S. soldiers also soured during Vietnam. According to most public opinion polls conducted during the years of heaviest fighting, a small majority of Americans believed the conduct of U.S. soldiers in Vietnam played a dramatic role in how the war was received.[83]

In October 2004, Paul Wolfowitz visited the Landstuhl Regional Medical Center, near Ramstein Air Base in Germany, which serves as a major U.S. military hospital for troops stationed from Europe to Southwest Asia. He met several young men and women who had been wounded in the Middle East by car bombs. One young sergeant had both legs broken when a bomb exploded while he was on patrol near Baghdad. In a touching moment captured by reporter Peter J. Boyer, Wolfowitz signed a copy of *Time* magazine that featured the American soldier as its "Person of the Year." Handing the soldier the autographed magazine, Wolfowitz reportedly looked the sergeant in the eye and said, "I'll tell you, no matter what people think about the war, ninety-eight percent of them love our soldiers. Period."[84]

There is no doubt Wolfowitz was correct about the change in attitude of the American public toward its soldiers. Even at the height of the Abu Ghraib prison scandal, public opinion polls across the nation showed the soldiers had the immense admiration of a large majority of Americans.[85] The polls suggest the empathy and sympathy created for the soldiers serving in Iraq—as compared with those in Vietnam—have been influenced by their older age, their volunteer status, their professional qualifications, and their closer resemblance to U.S. national demographics.[86] Another factor shaping this attitude is the presence of women in uniform in Iraq. Early in the war, a young woman from West Virginia—Jessica Lynch—captured the public's imagination. She came to symbolize the modern American army and all that was good about the U.S. mission. This added dimension created more empathy for the plight of soldiers in Iraq than was possible during the Vietnam War. Even as the public grows increasingly fed up with the aimless war in Iraq, people do not want to repeat the mistake of treating U.S. soldiers as badly as Vietnam-era troops were. Of course, Reagan-era revisionism about Vietnam and a general upsurge in the use of patriotic rhetoric in political elections have played a role in revitalizing the public's image of U.S. soldiers. Still, the American public overwhelmingly supports soldiers in Iraq and their families.

The problem for the Bush administration in Iraq, however, has never been lack of support for the troops. Rather, the problem has always been that massive U.S. military power has no political corollary. Despite the enormous differences between Iraq and Vietnam from an operational and strategic standpoint, the fundamental problem in both wars may be political: How does the United States win the hearts and minds of ordinary Iraqis? How does the United States increase the viability of the new government in Baghdad? Can Iraqi security forces provide the context for the government's political agenda to take root? Answers to all of these questions rest on the ability of the United States to have more success in nation building in Iraq than it did in Vietnam.

CHAPTER THREE

THE PROBLEMS OF NATION BUILDING

D URING a presidential debate with Vice President Al Gore in 2000, then-candidate George W. Bush declared, "I don't think our troops ought to be used for what's called nation-building."[1] Six years later, the biggest problem facing the United States in Iraq is not the insurgency but building a stable government in Baghdad. It will remain so for years to come for several reasons, not the least of which is that the Bush administration made absolutely no plans for post-Saddam Iraq. The Bush team believed it could quickly turn its limited invasion force into peacekeepers without addressing fundamental social, economic, and political problems in Iraq. That President Bush has refused to increase troop levels to maintain the peace shows a complete misunderstanding of the seriousness of nation building and its costs. As public pressure mounts for officials to announce a plan for troop withdrawals, as is likely to happen in Iraq as it did in Vietnam, Bush will face even more obstacles.

Because the Bush administration took to nation building so

hesitantly, the president admits that there are still significant problems to overcome. In January 2006, shortly after the Iraqi election of a new National Assembly, a more cautious President Bush warned that success in Iraq now would be up to the Iraqis themselves. He underscored this message in a series of policy speeches given that same month to bolster support for the war. He told a group of American veterans that "Iraqis still have more difficult work ahead."[2] That work includes building a strong army, creating a stable currency, reorganizing the central bank, guaranteeing property rights, establishing an impartial judicial system, improving local police forces, and making significant infrastructure improvements, all part of what some Bush insiders have called "the biggest nation-building experiment in history."[3] The president also hopes that constitutional reforms promised in the December 2005 national elections in Iraq will be able to bring Sunnis, Shiites, and Kurds together in a coalition government.

THE FUTURE OF IRAQ PROJECT

The Bush team apparently now understands the difficulties ahead, but it may be too late. Besides the enormous obstacles facing the U.S. effort in Iraq, there was the Bush administration's initial determined effort to ignore available expertise.[4] According to Paul Pillar, national intelligence officer on the Middle East 2000–2005, the administration purposefully ignored U.S. intelligence on the efficacy of war in Iraq and the problems of nation building there in order to pursue its larger agenda of democracy promotion. In a 2006 essay in *Foreign Affairs*, Pillar concluded the intelligence community sent the administration a message prior to the March 2003 invasion specifying that sanctions against Saddam Hussein promised the best success and that there was no pressing reason to go to war. Furthermore, the intelligence community warned the Bush administration that if the United States did go to war, it must "prepare for a messy aftermath."[5] In fact, the administration not only ignored the intelligence community on these pressing matters but also turned its back on experts that it had gathered to focus on the problems in Iraq.

From the earliest stages of the planning for war, the administration apparently was inclined to ignore the recommendations of the Future of Iraq Project, a group assembled by the U.S. State Department in early 2002 to help plan for a post-Saddam Iraq. The group included Iraqi exiles, experts from the State Department's Middle East Bureau, economists, security specialists, and political consultants. They met in a series of topical workshops designed to give the Bush administration the best thinking on nation building after the potential overthrow of Saddam Hussein. The project issued a number of specific reports, especially on the social aspects of nation building.

Shortly before the invasion of Iraq, however, the Pentagon took full control of the project, rejecting much of the already completed work. According to retired U.S. General Jay Garner, who took over the project at the Pentagon, Secretary of Defense Rumsfeld told him to "shelve" the Future of Iraq Project.[6] There had been significant debate between the State Department and the Pentagon over the project, but on the eve of the invasion, the Bush administration made the calculated decision to scrap the project in favor of its own military planners and what would become the Office for Reconstruction and Humanitarian Assistance (ORHA). Instead of focusing on the social and economic aspects of nation building, General Garner and

ORHA focused almost entirely on promoting democracy. For some, like Richard Perle, the former chairman of the Defense Policy Board, an influential group of advisers to the Pentagon, and Kanan Makiya, an Iraqi intellectual and adviser to the Iraqi National Congress, ORHA corrected much of the State Department's flawed thinking on nation building. According to Makiya, the State Department was interested only in meaningless social questions, such as how the United States could collect garbage in the streets the day after Iraqi liberation, or how Americans could recruit health care workers.[7]

For Perle and Makiya, the real problems were political. They were more interested in "big picture questions."[8] Perle has suggested that the State Department stood in the way of the Bush administration's plans for meaningful change in Iraq. He has argued repeatedly that the State Department and the CIA refused to engage Iraqis about the composition of the post-Saddam government and the transition to democracy. According to Perle, nation building would have been very successful in Iraq if the State Department had not been so parochial about what could be accomplished.[9] For Makiya, the State Department and the CIA were the biggest enemies of democracy in Iraq.[10] He was relieved, as was Perle, when the Defense Department took over the planning effort, and he believed Paul Bremer and his colleagues at the Coalition Provisional Authority (CPA) made up for lost time and missed opportunities.

THE RAND REPORT

Bremer followed through on many of General Garner's postwar plans, but he also introduced some new democracy programs supported by the Bush administration. As head of the CPA, Bremer endorsed the Rand Corporation's report "America's Role in Nation-Building: From Germany to Iraq."[11] Bremer called the study "a marvelous how-to manual for post-conflict stabilization and reconstruction." Furthermore, he declared, "I have kept a copy handy since my arrival in Baghdad and recommend it to anyone who wishes to understand or engage in such activities."[12] Bremer's colleagues in the Pentagon were equally impressed by the Rand report and followed many of its recommendations for postwar Iraq. For most Bush administration officials, whatever problems may have existed in planning and execution before Bremer's arrival in Baghdad were fixed by close adherence to the recommendations in the Rand study. Bremer's replacement, John Negroponte, also followed the Rand blueprint for success.

The Rand study called for sweeping changes in the political, economic, and security structures in Iraq. It suggested that the Bush administration take advantage of Iraq's existing nationwide civil administration, use the United Nations to help with humanitarian problems, and use Iraq's oil reserves to reduce Baghdad's dependency on foreign aid. The study also warned that the United States could not "afford to contemplate early exit strategies or leave the job half completed. The real question should not be how soon it can leave, but how fast and how much to share power with Iraqis and the international community while retaining enough power to oversee an enduring transition to democracy."[13] Rand also suggested that the United States mend its rift with its European allies because the nation-building project in Iraq would require multilateral action and cost sharing.[14]

What the Rand study does not mention, however, is Vietnam. Instead, it uses case studies from U.S. nation-building efforts in

Germany, Japan, Somalia, Haiti, Bosnia, Kosovo, and Afghanistan. A footnote to the study suggests that Vietnam was a "status quo" war, and that the U.S. nation-building effort was "too short" and "too limited" in its political objectives to warrant study.[15] Obviously, today's Rand researchers have forgotten that the Rand Corporation was at the very center of America's twenty-year effort at nation building in Vietnam. The Vietnam War was in many ways all about providing a stable government in Saigon as a counterrevolutionary alternative to Ho Chi Minh's Communists. The entire war rested on the viability of the Saigon government and its ability to convince its people that it was a legitimate, sovereign state. This is precisely what the Bush administration now faces in Iraq as it tries to convince Sunnis, Shiites, and Kurds to give up their separate political agendas for a unified, national one.

WHAT IS A NATION?

At the heart of any nation-building effort is the need to redefine for citizens what it means to belong to a nation. Scholars have been engaged in this exercise for decades, and some social-scientific reading is essential to an understanding of how to reconstruct Iraq. More than a decade ago, historian Benedict Anderson noted that nations are not natural entities but "imagined communities" requiring a great deal of blind faith. To him, the creation of nations is often a purely cognitive undertaking. Common languages, customs, and history are often imagined or constructed by civilians to strengthen bonds purposefully for survival.[16] Eric Hobsbawm picked up on Anderson's theme, suggesting that most traditions uniting disparate people into a nation are invented.[17] To Ernest Renan, the nation is a "large-scale solidarity, constituted by the feeling of the sacrifices that one has made in the past and those that one is prepared to make in the future." He concluded, however, that the single variable that ties people to a nation is the "desire to continue a common life."[18]

Michael Howard took a different approach. For Howard, the principle of nationalism has always been "indissolubly linked, both in theory and practise, with the idea of war."[19] Barbara Ehrenreich agreed. In her book *Blood Rites: Origins and History of the Passions of War*, Ehrenreich argued that the nation is "our imagined link to the glorious deeds—or the terrible atrocities still awaiting revenge—that were performed by others long ago." Her conclusion is that the nation is "a warrior lineage in which everyone can now claim membership."[20]

If past sacrifice and a desire to share a common future are at the crux of nationhood, it is no wonder the Bush administration is having such a difficult time in Iraq. Ethnic, tribal, religious, social, and political divisions are the hallmark of modern Iraqi history. Saddam Hussein held these disparate groups together only by brute force. Complicating matters for the Bush administration is the way Iraq became a modern nation-state. As historian Niall Ferguson and others have suggested, the Bush administration's difficulties today in nation building have their roots in the British experience in Iraq in the early twentieth century.[21] In 1914, when the British discovered Turkey was entering World War I on the side of the Germans, Prime Minister Lloyd George supported incursions into Iraq to secure key strategic areas for the British. General Charles Townshend launched a series of military raids into southern Iraq but failed in his initial attempts to take Baghdad. After two years of heavy fighting, the British finally captured the city. Arab allies connected with Husayn ibn Ali (the sharif of Mecca) led a revolt against the Ottoman Turks, helping Britain secure victory. At the end of the war, Britain established a new monarchy under the leadership of Ali's son, Prince Faysal. Britain then defined the national boundaries of Iraq with little regard for natural land constraints or traditional tribal and ethnic settlements, and this postwar policy produced the merger of Sunnis, Kurds, and Shiites into a modern Iraqi state. Now that Saddam is gone, the trick is how to hold these disparate groups together and to convince them that a future in common is in their best interest.

In Vietnam, in sharp contrast, the idea of nationhood held almost mythical qualities. Ho Chi Minh was fond of saying that Vietnam was "one nation and one people with four thousand years of history."[22] Although Ho seriously overstated the case, Vietnam indeed has had a long romance with its national history. Founded by migrating tribes from southern China, Vietnam has had a dependent but resistant cultural, social, and political relationship with its powerful northern neighbor. Throughout centuries of contact, Vietnam adopted many Chinese institutions and cultural and political habits, but it also created its own. Several independence movements depended upon the construction of an identity free of Chinese influence. In 40 CE, the Trung sisters avenged the death of a relative at Chinese hands by establishing the first independence movement in Vietnam. Although the Chinese quelled the rebellion three years later, the Trung sisters are still celebrated today in Vietnam as founders of a nationalistic independence movement dating back two thousand years. Their images can be seen throughout Vietnam, and one of the busiest streets in Hanoi still carries their name, Hai Ba Trung.

In the fifteenth century, Vietnam gained its full independence from China in a series of battles that now incorporate the country's most important national myth. In 1428, Le Loi, a wealthy landowner, led a revolt against the Ming occupation. Unsure of how to defeat his more powerful rivals, Le Loi went to a lake in the center of Hanoi to search for an answer. A tortoise came to him with a magical sword that could be used to defeat the Chinese only if it were returned to the lake. Le Loi took the sword, defeated the Ming overlords, and returned the sword to the lake. That lake now bears the name "Lake of the Restored Sword," and Le Loi is one of Vietnam's most celebrated national heroes, ascending to the throne as Emperor Le Thai To. For nearly 400 years, the later Le dynasty ruled Vietnam recounting the feats of Le Loi.

In the twentieth century, one of the keys to the Communist Party's success in Vietnam was its ability to convince ordinary citizens that the party was the keeper of the flame of nationalism. Beginning in the 1920s, leaders of the Vietnamese revolution linked the modern struggle to past sacrifices against foreign invaders. The party skillfully created national heroes out of those who sacrificed for the revolution. Celebration of this sacrifice gave the party preponderant power to assemble a pantheon of champions with ties to Vietnam's glorious past. Party publications stressed revolutionary continuity and national sacrifice.[23] One experienced reporter told fellow journalist Frances FitzGerald during the war that he finally realized the United States and its Saigon ally would never win "when I noticed the street signs in Saigon were named after Vietnamese heroes who fought against foreign invaders."[24]

The idea of a nation was central to Vietnamese revolutionary success, but so too was the construction of important symbols of national identity. Throughout the war against the Americans, Ho Chi Minh became one of those symbols. According to historian William

Duiker, the Communists used Ho's personality to "cement the Party's reputation as the legitimate representative of Vietnamese national tradition as well as the leading force in the Vietnamese revolution."[25] After Ho's death in 1969, he achieved cultlike status in Vietnam and around the world. He came to represent the aspirations of the nation, even if party handlers largely constructed his public persona. The party was so successful at disseminating its message of national unity that political training of citizens beyond the initial indoctrination program was usually not necessary. Ho's national narrative became a dominant fixture in the minds of PAVN regulars marching South.

From the earliest days of the revolution, Communist training manuals and political commissars made sure that PAVN and PLAF soldiers understood how the concepts of *dan toc* (nation, or the people) and *ai quoc* (patriotism, or love of country) merged to form a political ideology that put the cause of national liberation first. The PAVN and PLAF were organically connected to society, its leaders argued, and the Communists' support came directly from people in liberated areas. The connection to the national cause had been underscored throughout the basic training of Communist cadres and was constantly reinforced by political officers. At the heart of this training was the notion that the PAVN and PLAF were armies "of the people" that supported national liberation. In every phase of the revolution, therefore, the idea of nationhood was central.

An important—yet little known—aspect of the Vietnam War is that U.S. allies in South Vietnam also shared this sense of history. No political leader in Saigon denied that the people of both North and South Vietnam had a shared past and that cultural and ethnic homogeneity marked Vietnam's national history. Nguyen Cao Ky, South

Vietnam's vice premier, wanted to march north against Ho Chi Minh and his followers to unify the country under an anti-Communist banner. The political division at the seventeenth parallel between North and South Vietnam was a modern creation with no cultural or historical precedent. Most modern Vietnamese hold at least the perception that the country has a common language, common ancestry, and similar cultural practices. Although there are strong regional differences, the country has enjoyed a sense of unity from its earliest days. Despite U.S. efforts to create a new nation from dust south of the seventeenth parallel, most Vietnamese understood that the political contest in South Vietnam between Communist and non-Communist forces was in many ways a battle over who owned the past, and therefore the future, of Vietnam. Any nation-building effort had to begin with the premise that Vietnam was a unified nation with a long tradition of national political movements. That the United States and its allies failed to construct a lasting and victorious state does not detract from the fact that the Vietnamese people understood full well the idea of nationhood.

REBUILDING THE IRAQI STATE

In Iraq, the Bush administration now faces a very different historical and political situation from what Kennedy and Johnson faced in Vietnam. The goal, however, of building or reconstituting an independent and sovereign state is the same. The first task in nation building in Iraq, therefore, is bringing these disparate groups together. Borrowing a page from the Vietnam nation-building experience (perhaps without knowing it), the Bush team has argued that creation of a strong national army is the place to start. The thinking in Washington is that Iraqis need to provide for their own security but in a way that aids the nation-building process. The fear is that without a national army—the New Iraqi Army (NIA)—structured along U.S. lines and following U.S. training and operational procedures, each ethnic, religious, and tribal group would maintain its own security force. These forces would then be unleashed on each other to avenge rivalries formerly subsumed by Saddam's brutal use of force. A new national army would also serve the republican experiment in Iraq by providing a blueprint of what society could become: integrated and thinking along national lines. As the Bush administration continues to campaign for the viability of the NIA, the rhetoric is sounding much as it did during Vietnam-era administrations.

After the French decamped from Vietnam, the first action Americans took there in 1955 was to dismantle completely the Vietnamese National Army that had ties to the French colonial government. Nearly half the army inherited from the French was dismissed, and the United States went about creating the Republic of Vietnam Armed Forces (RVNAF) from scratch.[26] Lost in that transfer was years of experience fighting the Communists. Still, American military advisers believed it was better to start with a smaller army composed of U.S.-trained soldiers than it was to use an experienced army trained by France. In Iraq, the Bush administration also discarded experienced soldiers and officers when it created the NIA. Fearing that the army was made up of Baathist supporters of Saddam Hussein, the Bush administration gambled that it could create a new army that had no ties to the old regime. That gamble has had mixed results. Jeffrey Record, a historian writing for the Strategic Studies Institute, has labeled as a tragic mistake the CPA's decision in mid-

May 2003 to disband the entire Iraqi regular army with only a month's pay.[27] According to another source:

> The dismissal of Iraqi officers treated them as an extension of Saddam and the [Baathist Party's] rule . . . rather than as patriots who had fought for their country. It also added several hundred thousand men to the labor pool when there were virtually no jobs, and it effectively told all officers of the rank of colonel and above that they had no future in a post-Saddam environment. At the same time, it implied to all Iraqis that the New Iraqi Army might be so weak that Iraq would remain little more than a client of the United States and Britain in the face of the threat from Iran and possible future intervention by Turkey.[28]

Indeed, building an army from scratch is already difficult. Doing it in a time of war is nearly impossible. In both Vietnam and Iraq, U.S. military planners dismissed what could have been the bulk of a new national army, worried that it had ties to the old regime. The United States quickly learned in both instances, however, that those connections probably were not impossible obstacles to overcome.

In Iraq, this problem is particularly acute. According to Stephen Biddle, a senior fellow in defense policy at the Council on Foreign Relations, Iraq's Sunnis now see the NIA as a "Shiite-Kurdish militia on steroids."[29] The problem in a communal conflict, such as today's insurgent war in Iraq, is that the national army must represent all sectarian groups or it risks making any national government irrelevant. In Iraq, this means that the army has to mirror the major sectarian groups because the alliance of Shiites and Kurds "would hold real power regardless of what the constitution said."[30] Because Sunnis were cast out of the national army along with Saddam's Baathists, there is the growing feeling among many security experts in Iraq that they will never feel at ease in a coalition arrangement. Most Sunnis are unlikely to support the NIA and instead consider it the army of occupation. Finding a way to integrate Sunnis into the NIA remains one of the Bush administration's most pressing problems. If it cannot solve this conundrum, there may be no hope of building a coalition government and avoiding a bloody civil war.

TRULY NATIONAL ARMIES

As in Vietnam, another problem facing the Bush administration in Iraq today is getting the newly constituted army ready to assume a bulk of the military and security operations. In both wars, U.S. military officials launched an aggressive training program designed to bring the new armies up to speed as quickly as possible. In both cases, that process dragged on far longer than anyone in Washington had anticipated. With each passing month, U.S. military officials in Vietnam and Iraq understood the dangers of having Americans dominate military operations. Still, the new national armies were not ready to take on major responsibilities even after years of training. The dependency on U.S. armed forces to get the job done in Vietnam and Iraq slowed the nation-building process in both cases and threatened to destroy the credibility of those efforts. In both cases, the NIA and the RVNAF became an "army in waiting." And, in both cases, the wait lasted far longer than the national armies could afford.

In Vietnam, there were several significant problems with the training RVNAF forces received. Many of these problems led to poor performance on the battlefield and conflict with civilians. One of the most pressing issues was that tactical instruction programs were hampered by the lack of demonstrations or practical exercises and that training centers never had complete up-to-strength demonstration units commensurate with the large number of trainees.[31] When an operation required five experienced soldiers, the RVNAF troops saw it demonstrated with only two. Throughout the counterinsurgency era, demonstration units were often called away from their posts to put down a village uprising. Obviously, it is difficult to simultaneously fight today's insurgency and train tomorrow's soldiers. This is an age-old problem, one that will likely define the Iraq experience. There never seems to be enough time to train local forces to do the job that needs doing immediately.

Language and culture also provided impediments to successful training programs in Vietnam. American officers instructed in English using U.S. manuals. This was not a problem for most officers, but for enlisted men the language gap proved difficult to overcome. As for Iraq, how many U.S. training experts speak Iraqi Arabic, Najdi Arabic, Kurdish, Chaldean, or Assyrian? Even if training is handed over to Iraqi officers, as many administration officials insist is already happening, at some point in the training process an American must communicate about complicated goals and strategies with someone from a completely different culture. As the war dragged on in Vietnam, and strategic doctrine changed, many of the training manuals were not properly updated. Only in 2004 did the U.S. Army issue its new counterinsurgency training guide for soldiers in Iraq, the first since Vietnam. Outdated manuals, poor instruction, and the lack of live demonstrations can combine to undermine the training experience for everyone.

To compensate for insufficient training, U.S. advisers in Vietnam eventually instituted a combined operations program, sending RVNAF troops out with their U.S. counterparts.[32] Despite this program's success, it could not compensate for all the deficiencies in RVNAF training. Nor could it create confidence in South Vietnam's armed forces. The trend in Iraq is likewise toward more combined operations. There have been reports that U.S. troops will also mirror Iraqi police because of the many abuses in regional jails. If this is true, it is an alarming trend. A key element to success in building up national security forces is the "crossover point," where the national troops and police can assume a bulk of the operations. Despite public rhetoric to the contrary, events on the ground in Iraq suggest the United States is not sufficiently confident in Iraqi forces to hand over major security and policing responsibilities. Former Secretary of Defense Melvin Laird has argued that it is essential to reach this crossover point as soon as possible. In an essay in *Foreign Affairs,* Laird suggested that "the administration must adhere to a standard of competence for the Iraqi security forces." When that standard is met, U.S. troops "should be withdrawn in corresponding numbers."[33]

VIETNAMIZATION AND IRAQIZATION

Laird was prescribing for Iraq the old policy of "Vietnamization" used to pass more responsibility to the South Vietnamese armed forces. Laird's boss, Richard Nixon, described the policy this way: "We have adopted a plan which we have worked out in cooperation with the South Vietnamese for the complete withdrawal of all U.S. combat forces and their replacement by South Vietnamese forces on an orderly scheduled timetable. This withdrawal will be made from strength and not from weakness. As South Vietnamese forces become stronger, the rate of American withdrawal can become greater."[34]

U.S. strategy in Iraq is remarkably similar. President Bush hopes one day to turn over a majority of military and security operations to the NIA while withdrawing U.S. ground forces. The White House has been particularly optimistic in its predictions that the NIA can handle the job and that the time for the transfer of responsibility is drawing near.

After the December 2005 elections in Iraq, General Martin Dempsey, the U.S. commander of the Multinational Security Transition Command, said the crossover point was approaching. In a teleconference from Iraq, Dempsey reported roughly 100 battalions of Iraqi army soldiers were conducting security operations throughout the country and another 27 battalions of special police were providing a "bridge between combat and operations and civil police operations."[35] An Iraqi navy, an Iraqi border patrol, an Iraqi air force, and 75,000 Iraqi policemen joined these security forces. Despite the general's optimism, the Bush administration is not yet prepared to turn over major responsibilities to the Iraqis. In an important policy speech in January 2006, President Bush backed off on his earlier claims for withdrawal, suggesting that by the end of the year the goal was to have Iraqi security forces "control more territory than the Coalition."[36] The president also expected that the United States would withdraw two of the seventeen coalition brigades by June 2006, hoping that Iraqi security forces could make up the difference.[37]

The Iraqis, however, are experiencing difficulties in training. According to retired U.S. General Paul D. Eaton, who was in charge of training the NIA, poor planning, insufficient staffing, and inadequate equipment hampered the effort.[38] The general reported being dumb-founded when administration officials in May 2003, just one week after the president's "mission accomplished" speech, told him he would be sent to Baghdad to begin rebuilding the NIA. Immediately Eaton faced staffing problems. Promised 250 professional staff members, he began the training exercises with less than half that number. At no time during Eaton's eighteen months in Iraq did he have the proper staffing. He was also without adequate equipment to train the NIA. According to Eaton, he had to "scrounge" for even the most basic military supplies. "We were told to find anything we needed for the soldiers—boots, canteens, rucksacks, belts, beds, blankets" from Iraqi sources where possible.[39] Walter Slocombe, senior civilian adviser to the administration on national security and defense in Iraq, concurred with Eaton's assessment: "I have to agree with General Eaton, that it was hard to get the resources we needed out there. There was not a broad enough sense of urgency in Washington."[40] Of course, the decision by the Bush administration not to preserve any of Saddam Hussein's army exacerbated problems with training.[41]

Poor training usually leads to poor battlefield performance, and this was certainly the case in Iraq and Vietnam. In Iraq, the NIA's Second Battalion quickly dissolved after its initial contact with insurgents at Fallujah in April 2004. The Iraqi troops simply were not ready for combat or for criticism from locals. Some Fallujah residents called them "collaborators," and this had a devastating impact on troop morale. Although some important adjustments were made following the debacle at Fallujah, significant doubts remain about the viability of the NIA. Many military analysts fear that prematurely giving the NIA responsibility for the war against the insurgents will have damaging effects on Iraq's future. Others fear the NIA's dependency on U.S. troops is the most debilitating aspect of security operations in Iraq. All agree, however, that in January 2006, following the national elections, the Iraqi army was not yet ready to take over military and security operations completely.

In Vietnam, the RVNAF faced the same tough circumstances. During the first few years of the RVNAF's contact with PLAF regular infantry units, the South Vietnamese experienced significant defeats at Ap Bac, Song Be, and Ba Gia. Shortly after the battle of Ba Gia in 1965, the Intelligence Committee of the U.S. Mission in Saigon cabled Washington indicating that RVNAF losses at Song Be and Ba Gia were higher than expected.[42] The reports also suggested that the psychological toll of these defeats could lead to the "collapse . . . of the will to fight" on the part of the South Vietnamese forces, and that U.S. troops would probably have to be used to avert such a disaster.[43] On June 7, General William Westmoreland dispatched a long telegram to Washington outlining the difficulties:

> In pressing their campaign, the Viet Cong are capable of mounting regimental-size operations in all four ARVN corps areas, and at least battalion-sized attacks in virtually all provinces. . . . ARVN forces on the other hand are already experiencing difficulty in coping with this increased VC capability. Desertion rates are inordinately high. Battle losses have been higher than expected; in fact, four ARVN battalions have been rendered ineffective by VC action in the I and II Corps zones.[44]

Westmoreland saw "no course of action open to us except to reinforce our efforts in SVN with additional U.S. or Third Country forces as rapidly as practicable during the critical weeks ahead."[45]

Consequently, on June 7, 1965, Westmoreland requested an additional forty-four battalions (roughly 150,000 men) for Vietnam and permission to go on the offensive.[46] He believed he could halt Communist advances by deploying U.S. troops along the coast and near the major southern cities. He would then send units into the central highlands to block any Communist attempt to control Highway 9 (a major east-west road) and sweep to the sea in an effort to divide the country. After securing the coastal areas, the cities, and the highlands, Westmoreland believed he could then launch search-and-destroy missions with U.S. forces that would eventually grind down the enemy and diminish its will to continue the fight. The general would also rely on massive U.S. firepower, including the bombing of North Vietnam. Finally, the pacification effort in the countryside would provide enough local security for the government's programs to take hold.

President Johnson eventually agreed with Westmoreland's request. In spring and summer 1965, U.S. combat troops were introduced to Vietnam, and their operations shifted from mainly defensive to mainly offensive. With this change in policy and doctrinal thinking came a change in the relationship of the South Vietnamese army to the war and the nation. The official U.S. policy of assuming major offensive military missions unfortunately relegated the RVNAF to static defensive operations.

From 1965 until 1968, then, the South Vietnamese were passive actors in their own counterrevolution. This doctrinal shift signaled to RVNAF troops that their major benefactor did not think they could go toe to toe with the PAVN and PLAF. It was a demoralizing experience that had a dramatic impact on the conduct and outcome of the war. After taking over the war completely, the Johnson administration handed it back to the RVNAF in 1968, hoping to silence protesters in the streets at home and to rescue the 1968 election for Vice President Hubert Humphrey. Hoping to foster self-help and self-reliance for South Vietnam, Johnson began integrating RVNAF forces into major military operations with their U.S. allies. The process was accelerated in the Nixon years, but by then it was too late for the South Vietnamese to rally themselves. The Communists simply had too many military, political, and social advantages for the South Vietnamese to launch a successful counteroffensive.

In retrospect, it was a mistake for the United States to take over the Vietnam War completely. Over time, U.S. forces looked to much of the world like an occupying army, and the RVNAF lost confidence in its own ability to defend the nation. The Bush administration certainly faces the same problem in Iraq. The problem is how to balance security needs with Iraqi needs to provide that security themselves. Recent reports about ethnic divisions within the armed forces and the police in Iraq are not welcome news and point to the significant problems the Bush team faces in the coming years. What is clear, however, is that the Vietnam experience cannot be repeated. The United States needs to hand major security operations over to the Iraqis as soon as possible or the nation-building effort is sure to fail. If the Iraqi security forces cannot come together to form an alliance with common dreams and aspirations, is Iraq a nation at all?

Authoritarian rule was one of the few reasons for the success in Iraq of the fragile alliance created by the British at the end of World War I. From 1920 until 1958, the pro-British monarchy held disparate groups together by force and with massive amounts of British aid. There were constant protests and other signs of discontent throughout the pro-British period, but all were put down with force. In 1958, King Faysal II was overthrown by an anti-British, anti-Israeli coalition of pan-Arab supporters. One coup after another led to an increasingly unstable Iraq during the 1960s and early 1970s. Through it all, the Iraqi national armed forces tried to maintain political control and stability through the use of force. In 1961, Kurds in northern Iraq began a rebellion that many experts would argue continues to this day. When the Baathists took power in the 1970s, they promised to end the Kurdish rebellion and to put down the Shiite independence movement in southern Iraq. Saddam Hussein took control of the Baath Party and the country in 1979, increasing the Sunni hold on power. Hussein created a strong central state with a civil administration that was extremely loyal to the party. Hussein made little effort to bring Kurds and Shiites into the national government or the armed forces.

The United States is now facing an uphill battle as it tries to bring these disparate groups together through sheer force of will. Without a natural coalition against Iraq's enemies, Baghdad faces an uncertain future. Months after the national elections, considerable debate still swirls over the face of the government, especially the prime minister's office. Increased sectarian violence only adds to the likelihood that the government will not survive. Iraq may have had all the essential elements of a state in the twentieth century, but there is little evidence of nationhood. The army was never an army of the people but rather came to represent one sectarian group to the exclusion of others. Sunnis who once controlled the armed forces are now the subjects of its raids. Kurds have an increasing role to play in the national army, but they too remain outside the corridors of power. The history of modern Iraq does not inspire confidence in the ability of the state to convince its citizens of a shared national past with a common future.

SOCIOECONOMIC VIABILITY OF THE STATE

Compounding the problems in building up effective armed forces in Iraq, as in Vietnam, are serious political and social issues. In a protracted war, the socioeconomic viability of the state is more decisive than its ability to win or lose battles. Eventually, the government in Baghdad will have to deliver the goods, or it risks the same fate that met the Saigon government. During the Vietnam War, Saigon's inability to manage its own affairs ultimately proved just as devastating as Communist attacks. The Saigon government routinely spent 50 percent of its budget on nondefense-related items.[47] The United States supported these expenditures directly, but never provided enough maintenance to meet rising needs or costs. By 1965 the South Vietnamese deficit had mushroomed to unmanageable proportions, and inflation approached unprecedented levels. According to Jeffrey Clarke, the chief historian at the Center for Military History, consumer prices in South Vietnam rose 900 percent between 1964 and 1972. The cost of rice during this period rose an unbelievable 1,400 percent.[48] Military personnel on fixed salaries felt these economic strains intensely. During that same period, salaries of enlisted men rose only 500 percent, despite fifty redress actions.[49] RVNAF troops routinely complained about the lack of food, poor housing, overcrowded barracks, insufficient medical attention, and dismal pay.[50]

The rest of South Vietnamese society also felt these economic and social pressures. With rising inflation rates and a growing dependency on imports, the average citizen lost ground. Because of graft and corruption in the importation program, this once-proud exporter of foodstuffs now imported most items—even rice—at inflated prices. The government could do little to control inflation or the black market, and it lost the confidence of the people of South Vietnam quickly. Without massive amounts of U.S. aid, the South Vietnamese government would not have survived long on its own. The twenty-year nation-building experiment in Vietnam quickly grew into twenty years of extraordinary dependence, subsidies, price supports, economic credits, and kickbacks. Is this what is in store in Iraq?

The Bush administration believes Iraq is making substantial social progress and eventually its rich oil reserves will save it from dependency on U.S. aid. These optimistic predictions do little to change the fact that Iraq has serious social and economic problems. Reports of a booming economy are misleading, since most economic growth comes from foreign companies that have taken over newly privatized industries. Iraqi unemployment remains unusually high, and the inflation rate is staggering.[51] Foreign investment is improving, but primarily in foreign-owned or -operated entities. A basic question begs to be asked: Are Iraqis better off now than they were before the U.S. invasion? Scores of reports suggest the average Iraqi citizen is only slightly better off today than before the invasion, in economic and social terms. In several key areas, the U.S. nation-building effort has not produced the desired results. For example, the 2005 per capita income in Iraq was $3,400 per year, just ahead of Cuba. The unemployment rate during that same period was 25 percent, a figure that would be significantly higher if there weren't jobs in the U.S.-supported armed forces.[52] Finally, in 2005 only Zimbabwe had a higher annual inflation rate than Iraq's 40 percent.[53] Bob Herbert of the *New York Times* reported in early 2006 that despite the infusion of $16 billion in American taxpayer money, "virtually every measure of the performance of Iraq's oil, electricity, water, and sewage sectors has fallen below prewar levels."[54] Herbert's sources were U.S. government witnesses who testified before a U.S. Senate committee hearing.[55] Although there has been some improvement in a few vital social areas since the 2003 invasion, after three years of nation building, most Iraqis expect more.

Some critics of nation building, however, maintain the social aspects of the political war are overrated. Stephen Biddle has suggested that security is still the most important problem facing the Bush administration in Iraq. In his view, "survival trumps prosperity."[56] In an essay in *Foreign Affairs*, Biddle asked, "Would Sunnis really get over their fear of Shiite domination if only the sewers were fixed and the electricity kept working?"[57] This is an important question, one the Bush administration continues to wrestle with. If the Vietnam War is any guide, the president would be wise to develop social programs that integrated Sunnis, Kurds, and Shiites into a unified economy and national government if at all possible. At the end of U.S. involvement in Vietnam, Saigon was losing control of the population at an alarming rate. Failed social and political programs in South Vietnam quite possibly would have toppled President Thieu even without PAVN military advances. Proper sanitation and dependable electricity are important elements in any nation-building program. They are clear signs that the government is viable. Security is essential for these programs to take root, but ignoring the political war to concentrate only on security is a tragic mistake.

In retrospect, the Bush administration made a huge error in ignoring the U.S. intelligence community's warnings about the perils of nation building in Iraq and scrapping the recommendations of the Future of Iraq Project. The narrow focus on spreading democracy through military strength has led to several pitfalls. Today's U.S. armed forces are the best in modern history, but even they cannot alone carry the nation- building effort. As in Vietnam, Iraq needs a combination of security and social programs. In Vietnam, the United States took over the shooting war completely and left the political war to the South Vietnamese. The Saigon government failed miserably in addressing basic social and economic problems, and, as a result, it lost the confidence of its own people. The Communists were formidable adversaries, but the lack of social progress in South Vietnam doomed the nation-building experiment there. Even among those who understood the need to mix security with social programs, security came first. According to most policymakers in Washington, the United States had to provide enough security in South Vietnam for the social programs to take hold. It now seems clear, however, that security and social progress must proceed in tandem, or nation building cannot succeed.

After three years, finally there are signs the Bush administration and military planners in Iraq are beginning to understand the social needs of ordinary citizens. Major General Richard Zilmer and Lt. General Peter Chiarelli have started to emphasize the political war against the insurgents. For General Zilmer, U.S. commander of the dangerous Anbar province in Iraq, getting to know the needs of Iraqis has been one of his most important tasks. Along with providing security, the general now also makes sure that local health care workers and police officers are being paid enough to keep them on the job. He knows the ten largest employers in the province and is working closely with them to make sure they can continue to operate effectively. For General Chiarelli, reconstruction of the basic infrastructure goes hand-in-hand with providing security in Iraq. Both generals hope that promoting economic growth and development in the most impoverished areas of Iraq will dissuade Sunnis from joining the insurgency.[58]

Some in Washington wonder aloud if this emphasis on the political war and social issues has come too late.[59]

MODERNIZATION AS IDEOLOGY

In both Vietnam and Iraq, the social aspects of nation building rested upon a strong belief in modernization theory among key policymakers in Washington. During the cold war, many U.S. officials believed that newly emerging postcolonial nations could be brought into an alliance with the United States against the Communists through economic and political development. Social scientists working on problems of development in the 1950s, such as economist Walt Rostow, argued that modernization was a phased process that brought poor nations from subsistence to abundance and promoted freedom through a series of developmental stages that were common to all states.[60] At the most advanced stages were the United States and much of western Europe. Less developed countries, especially peasant societies in Latin America, Asia, and Africa, needed to follow the U.S. model, Rostow claimed, to advance to their fullest potential.[61]

Modernization was evolutionary, not revolutionary, the argument went, and it promised to free "backward" societies from the meddling of the Communists in Moscow and Beijing. Through careful political oversight and massive economic development aid, the United States could guide these newly emerging nations through the international minefield. At the core of Rostow's thesis was the belief that societies in the developing world would have to drop their traditional, ethnic-based practices and instead adopt Western structures and thinking. Lyndon Johnson's plan for a Mekong Delta project along the lines of a Tennessee Valley Authority to help Vietnam end the bonds of misery born out of material want was classic modernist thinking. He never fully understood that the purpose of the Communist revolution in Vietnam was to replace the very social structure Johnson wanted to impose there with a different one. The president favored a liberal capitalist blueprint for society, one the Marxists surely rejected. Modernization in the forms of direct foreign investment and a market economy would eventually come to Vietnam, but only after twenty years of contested cultural negotiations in Hanoi.

In Iraq today, the Bush administration faces many of the same modernization problems that plagued Kennedy and Johnson. Should Iraq develop its post-Saddam political and economic infrastructure along Western lines? Despite enormous efforts to ensure that the government and the economy fit the local cultural and social climate, many critics of the U.S. nation-building effort in Iraq think the Bush administration learned nothing from the U.S. experience in Vietnam, especially in the area of economic development. If Vietnam teaches anything in this realm, it is that billions of U.S. dollars in economic development aid is not enough to mend the problems of failed states. South Vietnam had very little to show for all the "modernization" that took place there. At the end of the day, economic development did little to stop the Communists or convince many South Vietnamese citizens to support the government in Saigon. If Iraq is to have a different fate, the Bush administration must pay attention to the pressing social issues brought forward by the Iraqis themselves.

THE STATE AND THE INDIVIDUAL

For average Iraqi citizens to embrace nation building, the government has to provide a meaningful outlet for political yearnings and act to protect civil and human rights. In Vietnam the lack of tangible democratic elections and a poor record on constitutional issues led citizens to view the government with suspicion. During the war, the government decided not to expand suffrage, and Saigon leaders did all they could to eliminate the political opposition from playing a role.[62] Despite U.S. efforts to the contrary, Saigon's officials believed their own personal power was more important than the nation-building experiment. Although never happy with the outcome, no U.S. administration protested the fixed elections in 1955, 1967, or 1971 or the antidemocratic nature of the government. The elections were little more than fig leaves to mask a seriously flawed political structure and successive administrations that failed to capture the support of the people. The people of South Vietnam certainly deserved better, and so do the people in Iraq.

Perhaps most damaging to the people of South Vietnam was the feeling that the political process was run by a small group of people connected to a secret party with its own security force. Throughout the war, the Can Lao Party controlled much of the political machinery in Saigon. Much like a nineteenth-century American political machine, the structure made it impossible for people to rise in politics or do business in South Vietnam unless they belonged to the Can Lao. The party had no recruitment drives or membership applications. Instead, party officials chose potential members. Once in power, the Can Lao ruled absolutely. From 1959 until the end of the war in 1975, citizens were routinely arrested without formal charges and held indefinitely. Can Lao officials often censored the press, and when editors refused to cooperate, their papers were shut down. Attacks against Buddhists by the largely Catholic Can Lao became legendary, but those attacks also extended to labor leaders and students. In short, any critic of the Can Lao–dominated government became an enemy of the state.

The lack of protected rights and the government's inability to deliver social goods eventually led the people of South Vietnam to turn their backs on the Saigon regime. Many subsequent revisionists of the war tend to blame Congress or the press for the U.S. defeat in Vietnam. It is important to remember, however, that long before Congress pulled the plug on funding the war, there was a lack of confidence in the government among the South Vietnamese. In the war's last months, President Nguyen van Thieu's government received a no-confidence vote from the National Assembly because of its inability to provide basic goods and services and his government's crackdown on civil liberties.[63] Rice wars erupted during the last two years of the war, since many South Vietnamese citizens lacked enough food to eat. Once an exporter of basic foodstuffs, South Vietnam had grown so dependent on U.S. imports and subsidies that it became an importer of key ingredients, even rice.[64] Throughout the war, ordinary citizens took to the streets in Hue, Da Nang, and Saigon to protest the government's lack of civil reform. The U.S. nation-building effort was doomed not only because of poor decision-making in Washington but also because the Saigon government failed to meet the needs of its people.

If Iraq is to have a different fate, the government in Baghdad will need to ensure its citizens' social progress and protect basic civil and human rights. Since the U.S. invasion, Iraq has had three elections and a new constitution has been established. There have been problems with each step, and the trick now is for the United States to disengage and give the Iraqis a chance to attack these problems for themselves. Their biggest political obstacle is how to increase participation and bring voices of opposition into the process. Reports from Iraq in January 2006 suggested the security police are less than impartial. Since Shiites dominate the police force, they can easily exact revenge on their Sunni neighbors. Many Sunnis complain regularly about police brutality and torture at the hands of the national police.[65] The Iraqi Islamic Party, the largest Sunni political group, claims the national police routinely round up its members. In some areas south of Baghdad, Sunni homes have been confiscated by the national police and redistributed to Shiite friends and families.[66] Some Sunnis fear the Shiite-dominated government in Baghdad will not reach out to its Kurdish and Sunni neighbors.

Perhaps the most trying issue facing the Bush administration is that its nation-building experiment in Iraq demands patience from the American public. The process of building strong civil-military institutions is arduous and time-consuming. Often, so few tangible results appear in the first years that the public can grow tired of waiting for success. The difficulty for Bush—as it was for Kennedy, Johnson, and Nixon—is that he has already spent considerable goodwill disproportionate to expected results. Once the gap between intentions and accomplishments widens, as it has in Iraq, the public begins to lose faith in what the administration has to say. After it was revealed that there were no weapons of mass destruction in Iraq, the public started to drift. When Bush officials claimed in early 2005 that the suicide bombers were the last gasp of the insurgency, the public started to question the efficacy of the war.[67] This issue has intensified as the bombings have increased.

If nation building is to be successful in Iraq, the Bush administration would be wise to review events in Vietnam carefully. The United States was so preoccupied with the appearance of democracy there that it did a poor job monitoring social and economic progress in a truly undemocratic state. Is it time to focus less on the noble goal of spreading democracy in the Middle East and more on social progress in Iraq? Are the two dependent upon each other, as the Bush administration believes? Some experts believe the Bush administration can back off its quest for total democracy in Iraq and save the government in Baghdad by emphasizing social progress and constitutional rights. In their view, the best export America can send to Iraq is not necessarily democracy but rather support for human and civil rights and social and economic progress. Journalist Fareed Zakaria has criticized the administration's insistence on transplanting democracy to Iraq as missing the point. In his view, Washington should accept a "liberal autocracy" in places like Iraq because this type of government can get the job of nation building done without the distractions of democratic politics.[68] Even the American version of democracy did not flourish overnight, he contends, and liberal autocracies might be able to deliver the social and economic programs needed for stabilizing the nation-building effort.

At the crux of this argument is the belief that constitutional protections of basic human and civil rights, combined with social and economic justice, might be more important than holding elections and having majority rule. Critics of the Bush administration point to the remarkable progress made in places like Taiwan, Singapore, Indonesia, and Thailand as proof that citizens might be willing to forgo democracy for a few decades in exchange for constitutional protections and economic progress.[69] It is an interesting argument, and one that will no doubt continue even after the dust has settled in Iraq. Many administration officials, however, doubt it is possible to have constitutional protections without democracy. As part of preparations for elections in Iraq, the Bush administration asked a group of U.S. and Iraqi experts on democracy and constitutional rights to oversee development of a series of laws to provide the blueprint for democracy and justice in Iraq. These experts operated under what became known as the Transitional Administrative Law (TAL). On March 8, 2004, the group submitted its recommendations.

The TAL called for the establishment of several democratic institutions in Iraq to support the nation-building effort there. It created a presidency council, a prime minister's office, and a congress with a system of checks and balances in place to ensure that no single entity controlled too much power. The presidency council held a veto power, but that veto could be overridden by the congress. The TAL also established an independent court system that protected basic civil liberties. No citizen could be held without charges, and every Iraqi had the right to a fair and speedy trial. The rights of all minority groups were preserved and protected by law and the independent judiciary. In short, the TAL promised many of the constitutional guarantees secured in the U.S. Constitution.

On December 15, 2005, Iraqis elected a 275-member Council of Representatives that will finalize a permanent constitution. Most Bush administration officials hope the new government will incorporate all of the TAL structures into the new constitution, and that probably will happen. But is mirroring the U.S. political and constitutional system the best thing for Iraq? In Vietnam, there were three national elections, two constitutions, a national assembly, and an independent judiciary. At no time, however, did a majority of the people of South Vietnam believe the government was viable. Despite an enormous nation-building effort by the United States over twenty years, Washington could never guarantee that these democratic institutions lived up to their responsibilities. Security issues overwhelmed all else. It was impossible to insist Saigon move on much-needed social reforms, because the war was going so badly in the countryside. In leaving the political war up to Saigon, the United States failed to ensure that pressing social and political issues were properly addressed.

In Iraq, the Bush administration's insistence that democracy be the cornerstone of any nation-building effort has meant that many social concerns likewise have been left for another day. Significant progress has been made on a number of fronts, but severe hardships still lie ahead. At some point, the Bush administration must permit the NIA to stand on its own, and the Iraqi security police will need to put aside ethnic and religious differences. All Iraqis must believe in a common future together if there is to be any hope of success. Social progress can help advance this process and is essential in any nation-building effort. But if the United States remains too long in Baghdad, Iraqis will meet the same fate that awaited South Vietnamese: growing social unrest, dependency, and resentment. Moreover, the American public will lose patience with nation building and the war in Iraq if there is no end in sight. Americans expect progress from the blood and treasure they expend. That is another lesson the Bush administration can learn from Vietnam.

CHAPTER FOUR

STAYING THE COURSE

A S THE BUSH administration was moving forward in its nation-building program in mid-2006, public support for the war was dwindling. As occurred for presidents involved in Vietnam, President Bush is ever-conscious of public opinion polls that clearly show Americans do not approve of the way things are going in Iraq. Blood speaks with a terrible voice, and Bush is no doubt experiencing the same agony Lyndon Johnson called his special burden.[1] Three times since 1945 Americans have been sent into harm's way when casualties were in the thousands—Korea, Vietnam, and Iraq—and each time public support for the war declined as deaths mounted.[2] As the insurgency in Iraq grows, and U.S. casualties rise, there will be more pressure to bring the troops home. It will be interesting to see how the Bush administration responds, but Vietnam will cast a long shadow over deliberations. Congressional members, too, hear the echoes of Vietnam as their constituents begin asking hard questions about the war.

The problem Bush faces in Iraq is similar to the problem Lyndon Johnson faced in Vietnam. In both cases, according to John Mueller, an expert on war and public opinion, the public gave substantial support to the effort as troops were sent in, but that support evaporated as the war dragged on.[3] In Vietnam, public opinion polls clearly showed that a majority of Americans supported Johnson's 1965 decisions to send combat troops there and to give them offensive missions.[4] Likewise, the Bush administration initially enjoyed enormous support from a majority of the American public when U.S. troops invaded Iraq.[5] In each case, however, public support declined sharply in the early stages of the conflict because reluctant supporters were quickly alienated.[6] Although the erosion slowed as approval was reduced to hard-core supporters of the war, overall public opinion never recovered to preinvasion levels. By 1967 less than half of the American people supported the war in Vietnam, and that remained the high-water mark for the remaining seven years of war.[7] For Mueller, Iraq is noteworthy because the decline in support has been faster than most experts predicted. In his view, this phenomenon has occurred because the American public "places far less value on the stakes in Iraq" than it did on those in Korea and Vietnam.[8]

According to Mueller, most Americans believe the perceived threats in Iraq—weapons of mass destruction and support for international terrorism—have been discounted.[9] Francis Fukuyama of Johns Hopkins University's Paul Nitze School of International Affairs, agrees, adding that with those justifications gone, the war in Iraq has become a request to spend "several hundred billion dollars and thousands of American lives in order to bring democracy to . . . Iraq."[10] Most Americans simply do not share the Bush administration's enthusiasm for planting the seeds of democracy in the Middle East. Mueller concludes that the remaining public support for the war probably comes from those who still believe there is a connection between events in Iraq and international terrorism.[11] As suicide bombers in Iraq become better known and their motives clarified, even this support might decline.

The Bush administration did learn some lessons from Vietnam. Since the invasion of Iraq began, officials have worked tirelessly to keep body bags and flag-draped American coffins from public view. This and the absence of a draft probably have kept thousands of young people from marching in the streets, but public support is still waning. The press has not been as hostile to Bush as Kennedy, Johnson, and Nixon claimed it was to them, and Congress has done little to rein in the administration in Iraq. During Vietnam, Congress made several attempts to limit the president's ability to wage war, and the U.S. Senate Foreign Relations Committee held important hearings that brought various critics of the administration's actions to testify before the nation, including George F. Kennan, the father of the original containment policy. By the war's end, Congress passed the War Powers Act, which severely limited the president's actions in war. Specifically, the legislation required the president to inform Congress within forty-eight hours of the deployment of U.S. military forces abroad and to withdraw them within sixty days unless Congress approved an extension. Critics of U.S. policies in Iraq claim President Bush has had unfettered power compared with Vietnam-era presidents.

PROMOTING THE WAR

President Bush does sound like Lyndon Johnson when he is on the stump trying to rally support for the war. Bush often places Iraq in the context of past American struggles for freedom and independence. He has stated frequently that Iraq is the next phase of the

American freedom struggle. Like President Johnson, Bush is also fond of using soaring rhetoric to describe the U.S. commitment to Iraq. One of Johnson's favorite tactics was to sell the war to American citizens by appealing to their ideals. For example, he often claimed that the principle at stake in Vietnam was the same as that "for which our ancestors fought in the valleys of Pennsylvania."[12] Vietnam, the president declared, was not a war about territory; it was a war to usher in a new era of Asian economic and political development to end "the bondage of material misery" in that part of the world.[13] Johnson was also fond of asserting that most countries would shrink from the burden of responsibility the United States faced in Vietnam. He lauded America as the "strongest and greatest democracy on earth" and said only the United States had "the intelligence, the resources, and the will to endure a distant struggle for freedom's sake."[14] Johnson usually ended his policy speeches with some version of this refrain: "We will not be defeated. We will not grow tired. We will not withdraw, either openly or under the cloak of a meaningless agreement. We must stay in Southeast Asia—as we did in Europe—in the words of the Bible: 'Hitherto shalt thou come, but no further.'"[15] Substitute "Iraq" for "Southeast Asia," and the two Texans sound very much alike.

The problem with appealing to ideals, however, is that such appeals eventually must be grounded in national security interests, or the nation grows increasingly impatient. During Vietnam, it became more difficult to convince ordinary Americans that all the fighting and dying were worth it. Although most Americans supported intervention in Vietnam in 1965 to stop the spread of communism, by 1967 they no longer believed that goal was of primary importance to U.S. national security. In the absence of an overarching idealistic framework for the war, public support melted away. Saving South Vietnam did not carry the same cachet as saving the world from communism, and too few Americans believed Vietnam was worth the sacrifice. Johnson's appeal to ideals, much like Bush's today, ran its course, and Americans eventually concluded the troops should be brought home.

THE CREDIBILITY GAP

The public also lost confidence in the Johnson administration's ability to close the gap between intentions and accomplishments. At the height of the war, when most Americans realized things were not going well in Vietnam, Johnson launched a public relations campaign designed to convince them otherwise. Westmoreland, who returned home in November 1967 to shore up support for the war, appropriately fired the first volley. Upon arriving in Washington, Westmoreland told reporters, "I am very, very encouraged. . . . We are making real progress." In an important speech before the National Press Club, the general was even more optimistic. He concluded the enemy was badly hurt and the war had "reached an important point where the end begins to come into view."[16] He hinted substantial troop withdrawals would be possible within two years.

While Westmoreland made the rounds in Washington, Johnson organized several committees to go out and promote the war's progress.[17] The president formed the Committee for Peace with Freedom and the Vietnam Information Group to monitor public support and tackle problems as soon as they surfaced. These groups reported the major obstacle facing the president was the public's misperception that the war was a stalemate. Accordingly, Johnson ordered both groups and the U.S. embassy in Saigon to "search urgently for occasions to present sound evidence of progress in Vietnam."[18] The publicity machine went into high gear, promoting stories about PAVN/PLAF body counts and significant military victories in the Mekong Delta, the heart of the insurgency. For a brief period at the end of 1967, it appeared as if the public relations offensive had worked. Polls showed that support for the war, though below 50 percent, was holding steady.[19] The mood in the White House became optimistic for the first time in years.

The events of January 30, 1968, shattered Johnson's hope of fixing the public opinion problem. Early that morning, combined PAVN and PLAF forces attacked six major cities, thirty-six of the forty-four provincial capitals, sixty-four district capitals, and fifty hamlets in what became known as the Tet offensive.[20] Although Communist forces suffered huge military losses and did not achieve the general uprising many party strategists had hoped for, the offensive was a key turning point in the American public's support for the war. Live television accounts of the battles in key cities, such as Hue and Saigon, convinced American viewers that Johnson and Westmoreland had been deceiving them. Overnight, support for the war fell by nearly 20 percent.[21] Even the venerable television anchor Walter Cronkite, an initial supporter of the war, wondered aloud if the Johnson administration had been misleading the American people. "What the hell is going on?" Cronkite asked. "I thought we were winning the war!"[22]

THE MYTH OF A LIBERAL PRESS

For many Americans, however, Tet and its treatment pointed to what was wrong with the press and its reporting and not what was wrong with the war. Revisionist histories today incorrectly argue that the "liberal media" purposefully distorted events during the Tet offensive to promote an antiwar message.[23] Some believe the same could happen in Iraq. Morton Krondracke, a Washington columnist, has argued that the media could indeed snatch defeat from the jaws of victory in Iraq if they are not constrained. He uses the Tet offensive and the war in Vietnam as his parallels. Krondracke believes Tet was a military defeat for the Communists, but the media spun it a different way: "The U.S. media reported the episode as a U.S. defeat, helping convince the American establishment that the war was unwinnable." In his view, a real danger is "that Iraq could become like Vietnam—a self-inflicted defeat."[24] Although the Communist Party did not achieve some of its stated goals during Tet, the Western press had little to do with the outcome of the war. Hanoi's ability to determine the scope and place of battles and to win peasants to its side had very little to do with press reports.

The Abu Ghraib prison scandal is a favorite topic for those who think the press is going too far and being too negative in its reporting of events in Iraq. Most critics of the media feel they fixate on negative stories and do not understand the harm they are doing to the American cause. Several press opponents have argued that reporters, especially U.S. reporters, should get on the team.[25]

For those old enough to remember Vietnam, this may sound eerily familiar. On January 2, 1963, RVNAF forces from the army's 7th Division attacked the PLAF's 261st Main-Force Battalion at the tiny hamlets of Bac and Tan Thoi, located sixty kilometers southwest of Saigon. Though outnumbered and outgunned, the PLAF stood its ground, shooting down five U.S. helicopters and retreating under cover of darkness without suffering high casualties. The

South Vietnamese, in embarrassing contrast, refused to advance under fire and lost sixty men.[26]

In ensuing days, readers of English-language wire services and newspapers were given their first solid indication that Military Assistance Command–Vietnam (MACV) reports on the war had been overly optimistic and that something had gone terribly wrong. Reporting for United Press International, Neil Sheehan first heard about the debacle in the early afternoon of January 2, 1963. That evening, he and Nick Turner of Reuters took a motorcycle to Tan Hiep, a command post in the northern delta. There, in the darkness, John Paul Vann, the U.S. adviser attached to RVNAF who fought at Ap Bac, described the battle scene. He told reporters a number of mistakes were made, and the PLAF "were brave men" who gave a "good account of themselves today."[27] The next day, David Halberstam, writing for the *New York Times*, joined Sheehan and Turner at the Tan Hiep command post. The young reporter asked Vann, "What the hell happened?" Vann replied candidly, "A miserable damn performance, just like always."[28] Sheehan and Halberstam filed their reports and changed the nature of the relationship between the press and the military high command in Vietnam forever.

Sheehan's account was the most detailed, suggesting that Ap Bac was a "major defeat" and symptomatic of larger problems in Vietnam.[29] On January 7, the *Washington Post* ran Sheehan's story on the front page: "Angry United States military advisers charged today that Vietnamese infantrymen refused direct orders to advance during Wednesday's battle at Ap Bac and that an American Army captain was killed while out front pleading for them to attack."[30] For five consecutive days, Halberstam's stories appeared on page one or two of the *New York Times*. The headlines told the story: "Vietcong

Downs Five U.S. Copters, Hits Nine Others";[31] "Vietnamese Reds Win Major Clash";[32] "Vietnam Defeat Shocks U.S. Aides."[33] Sheehan's and Halberstam's reports contradicted the most optimistic predictions from the Kennedy White House and suggested the public was not "getting the facts on Vietnam, even at this time when American casualties are mounting."[34]

A few days after the negative press reports, Admiral Harry Felt, commander in chief of the U.S. Pacific Command (CINCPAC), flew from Hawaii to Saigon for an inspection tour. When he met with reporters his first night there, he said he did not believe "what he had been reading in the papers." Instead, he insisted Ap Bac "was a Vietnamese victory—not a defeat, as the papers say."[35] Felt called Ap Bac a victory, he later reported, because the NLF had abandoned the area to the ARVN's 7th Division.[36] General Harkins supported Felt's assertions, claiming the ARVN had "taken the objective."[37] Savvy journalists questioned the logic of these statements: Most knew this was not a war about territory. Halberstam, recounting the surreal experience some months later, wrote: "We were all stunned at these new rules for guerrilla warfare—evidently the objective now was terrain, not the enemy."[38] Malcom Browne of the Associated Press was so infuriated by Felt's comments that he challenged the military leader's understanding of guerrilla war. Felt's angry response was, "Why don't you get on the team?"[39]

Is history repeating itself? Probably not, but the administration's relationship with the press is crucial during a time of war. Every Vietnam-era president complained the media were against him and were reporting events unfairly. Lyndon Johnson believed the press was the pulse of the American people, commenting once that if he had lost support of journalist Walter Lippmann, "he had lost America."[40] Lippmann, a one-time supporter of the president, turned against Johnson and the war in early 1966. In one particularly harsh column, Lippmann wrote, the president had "never defined our national purpose except in the vaguest, most ambiguous generalities about aggression and freedom."[41] Many Americans agreed, and Johnson's approval rating reflected that fact. From the introduction of U.S. ground troops in March 1965 until the day he left the White House in January 1969, Johnson's public opinion polls and support for the war dropped steadily.[42]

Not everyone agreed with public opinion polls on the Vietnam War. President Richard Nixon believed there was a "great silent majority" of Americans who still supported the war and would back his policies. In his mind, the vast majority of Americans did not support the antiwar protesters and instead understood the stakes in Vietnam. In a November 1969 speech, Nixon tried to isolate his critics and regain popular support for the war by charging that the antiwar movement was "irrational" and "irresponsible."[43] He called on the "great silent majority" to support Vietnam in its hour of need and issued a dramatic conclusion aimed at the protesters: "North Vietnam cannot humiliate the United States. Only Americans can do that."[44]

President Bush has made a similar charge, suggesting that those in Congress who speak out against the war and label as faulty the intelligence that led to it are "unpatriotic."[45] Bush has also lashed out at members of Congress for making the Vietnam analogy, saying the comparison is false and "sends the wrong message to the enemy."[46] Similar refrains were heard during Vietnam, and many members of the Nixon White House criticized the antiwar protesters for aiding and abetting the enemy. The White House went after its enemies, compiling a list of names to be targeted for investigation and placing wiretaps on many civilians.

GROWING RESISTANCE TO THE WAR

Much as during the Vietnam era, a mood is growing in Congress that the president has overstepped his constitutional authority, and this mood deepened especially after revelations about the Bush administration using wiretaps without legal warrants.

Some members of Congress have openly likened Iraq to Vietnam. In April 2004, during a period of particularly heavy American and Iraqi casualties, U.S. Senator Edward Kennedy (D-Mass.) declared in a Washington speech, "Iraq is George Bush's Vietnam."[47] During a subsequent television interview, Kennedy said, "We're facing a quagmire in Iraq, just as we faced in Vietnam." He particularly cited the lack of information: "We didn't understand what we were getting ourselves into in Vietnam. We didn't understand what we were doing in Iraq. We had misrepresentations about what we were able to do militarily in Vietnam. I think we are finding that out in Iraq as well."[48] Kennedy's comments helped convince others to speak out. Senator Harold Ford Jr. (D-Tenn.) also saw similarities between Iraq and Vietnam, concluding, "The gnawing and growing feeling that the goal of achieving U.S.-style democracy in Iraq is unattainable is reminiscent of the feeling that gripped America during Vietnam."[49] His colleague, Robert Byrd (D–W.Va.), rose on the Senate floor to say, "Now, after a year of continued strife in Iraq, comes word that the commander of forces in the region is seeking options to increase the number of U.S. troops on the ground if necessary. Surely I am not the only one who hears echoes of Vietnam."[50]

Indeed he was not. Several national publications jumped on the Vietnam bandwagon, including *Newsweek*, which ran "The Vietnam Factor" on its April 19 cover. Bob Herbert of the *New York Times* claimed the United States was repeating the Vietnam experience in Iraq. "We have been there, done that, and now we are doing it again," he wrote in an editorial in September 2004.[51] His colleague at the *Washington Post*, Robert Kutner, editorialized that the Iraq conflict "is becoming more and more reminiscent of the Vietnam disaster. American troops mostly stay in heavily fortified barracks. When they do venture out, their sweeps don't achieve durable pacification. Militants and young men of fighting age are long gone by the time American bombardments start."[52] Lawrence Freedman, professor of war studies at King's College in London and one of the most respected military historians in the world, wrote, "Just as Vietnam became McNamara's war, Iraq has become Rumsfeld's war."[53]

In November 2005, House member John Murtha (D-Penn.) stunned his colleagues by calling for the immediate withdrawal of U.S. troops from Iraq. Murtha, one of the top House Democrats on military spending, said U.S. troops were the primary target of the insurgency and Americans had become a "catalyst for violence."[54] In a speech reminiscent of the intense Vietnam-era debates in Congress, Murtha concluded it was time to bring the troops home.[55] The usually hawkish Murtha set off a firestorm in Washington that concluded with a Senate vote to press the Bush administration for concrete steps toward troop withdrawals but drew (sharp) protest from Vice President Cheney. Cheney told reporters that politicians who compared Iraq to Vietnam and criticized President Bush were engaging in "dishonest and reprehensible" behavior.[56] Murtha fired back about "guys who got five deferments and [have] never been there and send people to war, and then don't like to hear suggestions about what needs to be done."[57] Cheney did not serve in the military, whereas Murtha is a highly decorated Vietnam veteran.

Another Vietnam veteran, William Nash, a retired U.S. Army major general who also served in the Persian Gulf and Bosnia and is a senior fellow at the Council on Foreign Relations, has found Iraq and Vietnam eerily similar. In his view, the United States is once again fighting a protracted war with the wrong tactics. "Now we have Vietnam [in Iraq]. You've got a sovereign government over there, a big embassy, and 140,000 U.S. soldiers. And our ability to influence political decisions is finite."[58] Similar comments have come from Anthony Zinni, a fellow Vietnam veteran who also served with U.S. forces in Somalia and who preceded Tommy Franks and John Abizaid as chief of Central Command in the Middle East. Zinni has noted a similarity between Iraq and Vietnam because in both cases overall military strategy is flawed: "Some strategic mistakes are very similar," and in both cases the White House is trying to "draw the American people into support of the war by cooking the books. We did it with the Gulf of Tonkin situation . . . and here we have had the case for WMD [weapons of mass destruction] as an imminent threat for not using international authority to go in."[59]

Even supporters of the war in Iraq are drawn to the Vietnam analogy. Senator John McCain (R-Ariz.) has repeatedly used the debacle in Vietnam as evidence that the United States needs to send more troops to Iraq. Early in the war when Secretary Rumsfeld claimed that 132,000 U.S. troops could defeat the insurgency in Iraq, an angry McCain publicly disagreed, stating, "The simple truth is that we do not have sufficient forces in Iraq to meet our military objectives." McCain concluded his remarks with a prophetic warning that if the

United States did not send more troops, it would risk "the most serious American defeat on the global stage since Vietnam."[60] Several other Republicans have joined McCain in calling for more troops, arguing that in their absence the United States will face "another Vietnam."[61] Senator Chuck Hagel (R-Neb.), a Vietnam veteran and often considered one of the most conservative Republicans in Congress, has criticized the war from its very beginning.

CONGRESSIONAL CRITICS

Hagel's protest is unusual, though, as few Republicans have broken ranks with the president over the war in Iraq. According to some public opinion experts, the partisan divide over the war in Iraq is considerably greater than for any U.S. military action over the past half century.[62] Furthermore, as political scientist Gary Jacobson noted, President Bush's overall approval rating is also more partisan than the rating for any president over that period, including Bill Clinton, Ronald Reagan, Jimmy Carter, and Richard Nixon.[63] The president, therefore, has won all the support he can expect from his fellow Republicans in Congress and across the nation. Democrats see the war in Iraq as one of the major election issues. The partisan divide, however, is not likely to change how the public feels about the conduct of the war. Whatever support the Bush administration had in early 2006 following the national elections in Iraq is probably the high-water mark it can enjoy for the remainder of the war, no matter how successful the nation-building effort is in Baghdad.

Lyndon Johnson did not even receive partisan support for his policies in Vietnam. During Johnson's five years in office, his most strident opponents often were members of his own party and usually former Senate colleagues. Richard Russell (D-Ga.), Mike Mansfield (D-Mont.), and J. William Fulbright (D-Ark.) became outspoken critics of Johnson's war. Fulbright charged that under Johnson's presidency, the United States had fallen victim to the "arrogance of power." He argued that Washington was showing "signs of that fatal presumption, that over-extension of power and mission, which brought ruin to ancient Athens, to Napoleonic France and to Nazi Germany."[64] Other liberals in Congress questioned the significance of Vietnam, asking if it was indeed vital to U.S. national security interests. Furthermore, they argued that the high cost of the war was diverting attention from more urgent social problems at home, hoping to revive Johnson's attention to his own Great Society program.[65] Some in Congress challenged Rusk's view that the United States needed to stay the course in Vietnam to convince its allies it honored its commitments.[66] Indeed, these dissenters suggested the British, French, and Germans opposed the war and wanted the United States to announce a withdrawal.

Johnson had conservative critics as well. Several conservative members of Congress charged the president was not "fighting the war to win."[67] They believed the war in Vietnam was crucial to the larger cold-war struggle. If the United States did not succeed in Vietnam, they feared the Communists would take this as a signal that America was weak and that other newly emerging postcolonial nations were up for grabs. These hawks viewed antiwar demonstrators with suspicion, and some believed the press had a liberal bias.[68] Most argued that Johnson was preventing the military from doing what it did best—fighting and winning wars. Many said McNamara and his civilians at the Pentagon were wrong to limit the war, and some in Congress openly challenged the president to attack North

Vietnam directly, no matter the consequences.[69] Representative Mendel Rivers, a conservative Democrat from South Carolina, told the president to "win or get out," summing up the feeling of many in Congress.[70]

Johnson focused much of his attention on his conservative critics, an emphasis that might have cost him his presidency. When public opinion and much of Congress turned against the war in early 1967, Johnson still tried to appease his conservative challengers. He rejected Westmoreland's 1967 request for an additional 200,000 troops, and he rebuffed McNamara's proposal to limit or stop the bombing. To placate the conservatives and his own Joint Chiefs, Johnson significantly expanded the list of bombing targets, and for the first time authorized strikes against bridges, railways, and military barracks near Hanoi, Haiphong, and the Chinese border. By trying to stand firmly on the middle ground, however, Johnson wound up alienating his base of support, southern Democrats and liberals. In retrospect, Johnson might have been well advised to pay more attention to the antiwar protesters and his own party. When public opinion turned solidly against the war and his presidency after the January 1968 Tet offensive, he had little choice but to step aside and let another Democrat represent the party in the November presidential elections.

Richard Nixon also had difficulty keeping Congress and public opinion behind his Vietnam programs. As with Johnson, many of Nixon's critics came from his own party. One of the most outspoken was Jacob Javits, a Republican senator from New York. Javits criticized Nixon for doing little to end the war.[71] He insisted the president pay serious heed to public opinion polls that suggested most Americans supported an immediate withdrawal from Vietnam. After the Nixon administration invaded Cambodia in spring 1970, several

Republicans in the Senate cosponsored resolutions that, if passed, would have severely limited the president's power in Vietnam. In June 1970 the Senate voted overwhelmingly to terminate the 1964 Gulf of Tonkin Resolution that had granted Lyndon Johnson unusual presidential power to wage war. Senators John Sherman Cooper (R-Kent.) and Frank Church (D-Idaho) cosponsored an amendment to cut off all funds for U.S. military operations in Cambodia by June 1970. Mark Hatfield, a Republican from Oregon, cosponsored a bill with the liberal George McGovern (D–S.D.) that would have required the Nixon administration to withdraw all U.S. forces from Vietnam by the end of 1971. Although none of these restrictive measures passed either house of Congress, it was clear by 1970 that Congress no longer supported the war in Vietnam.

Eventually, Nixon's enemies in Congress far outnumbered his friends. Even before the 1972 Watergate scandal, the president faced growing opposition to his Vietnam policies. On two separate occasions, the Senate approved binding resolutions that would have required the president to remove all U.S. troops from Vietnam by a specific date if Hanoi cooperated on the release of U.S. prisoners of war. In both cases, the House removed the deadline and watered down the resolution. Still, Nixon knew his hands were tied. Even though he and his national security adviser, Henry Kissinger, assured the South Vietnamese leadership in Saigon that the White House would see the war to the bitter end, both men knew clearly by 1971 they had little support for extending the war much further. It was only a matter of time before Congress, acting on the wishes of the American people, would cut funding for the war or demand a complete U.S. withdrawal.

THE CREDIBILITY FACTOR

As public support for the nation-building effort in Iraq dwindles, the Bush administration can expect Congress to pressure it to announce plans for a troop withdrawal. Just as in Vietnam, the president will face increasing criticism from Congress as the war's costs mount. And just as Johnson did before him, President Bush also faces opposition to withdrawal from some conservatives, many of whom form the core of his support base. They contend a premature U.S. withdrawal will precipitate a bloody civil war in Iraq. In their view, the president must establish more of a military presence in Iraq, not less. Like Johnson, then, Bush is feeling pressure both from Democrats and Republicans in Congress. And in another parallel to Vietnam, the middle ground in Iraq is shrinking and perhaps even becoming an untenable position to maintain. If the Vietnam War is any guide, fear of the consequences of withdrawal is perhaps the most paralyzing factor facing the Bush administration today.

During the Vietnam War, the fear of what might happen in South Vietnam and to American credibility if the United States withdrew kept the nation bogged down. President Johnson complained repeatedly that he could not "get in deeper" and that he could not "get out."[72] At the heart of that conundrum was the realization that withdrawal carried with it some painful consequences. The Bush administration has accepted Colin Powell's formulation of the problem. Borrowing from Pottery Barn (though he denies the attribution), Powell said: You broke it, you bought it. In other words, many key people on the Bush team think withdrawing from Iraq before the job is done borders on the criminal because the United States introduced instability with its invasion. In sum, Washington must see the process through until an independent Iraq can stand on its own. A certain circular logic to this justification is indeed reminiscent of the Vietnam War.

Lyndon Johnson frequently insisted the United States could not simply withdraw from Vietnam because U.S. credibility was on the line.[73] American prestige was at stake in the jungles of Vietnam, Johnson reasoned, and he was not going to let down his allies. Johnson feared other nations around the world would no longer trust the United States if it withdrew from Vietnam. How ironic, then, that it was Johnson's European allies, nations whose trust and confidence carried such weight among administration officials, who turned against the war and U.S. policy in Vietnam. From early 1962, leaders in NATO-allied France, Germany, and Britain argued for a neutralist settlement to the crisis in Vietnam and a U.S. withdrawal.[74]

Johnson neither heeded their advice, nor in fact even heard what they were saying. Instead of withdrawal, Johnson tried to convince his European allies to join him in the fight in Vietnam. He called his coalition of the willing the "many flags approach."[75] The problem for Johnson, however, was that not one European ally agreed with the U.S. position in Vietnam. An angry Johnson once begged British Prime Minister Harold Wilson to send at least one "British cook to Vietnam" so that the United States could claim its allies supported its Vietnam policy.[76] When Wilson refused, Johnson bellowed, "Maybe you never got your copy" of the SEATO treaty, requiring Britain and the United States to defend South Vietnam.[77] Wilson's response was to publicly criticize U.S. bombing raids over North Vietnam and suggest the United States seek a negotiated settlement.

Of course, Johnson was also concerned about personal credibility. Much of what drove him was the desire not to be the first president to lose a war.[78] He was especially fearful of the difficulties Harry

Truman and the Democratic Party faced over charges in 1949 that the president had "lost China." After Mao's victory in China, Congress had erupted in accusations that Truman had been "soft on communism" and "asleep at the wheel."[79] Johnson would not let a debate over Vietnam wreak similar damage on his administration. Such a debate, Johnson concluded, "would shatter my presidency, kill my administration, and damage our democracy."[80] Above all, Johnson feared conservative members of his own party, especially powerful southerners in key congressional leadership positions, would "push Vietnam up my ass every time" if he did not intervene and South Vietnam was eventually lost.[81] Obsessed with not appearing weak, Johnson often repeated he was not going to be the first president to "turn tail" and run or "be shoved out of a place."[82] No, Johnson concluded, "We've got to conduct ourselves like men."[83]

This mixture of international and personal credibility fueled much of the fire over Vietnam. The United States had to intervene in Vietnam to show its allies it lived up to its treaty commitments. Once engaged, there was no easy exit. Senator George Aiken (R-Vt.) once suggested the United States simply declare victory in Vietnam and go home. Considerable support existed in Congress for withdrawal, but there were also members who believed Johnson had to "get in deeper" to win. The Joint Chiefs continually pressed the president to widen the war by mining Haiphong harbor and increasing the bombing around Hanoi and the Ho Chi Minh Trail. Johnson rejected these suggestions, but he clearly felt pressure from both sides to settle the Vietnam issue once and for all.

By 1967 several of Johnson's key supporters and advisers no longer believed the "psychological domino theory" should keep the United States in Vietnam. The first dissenter was Robert S. McNamara. As early as 1965, the defense secretary had doubts about the efficacy of the military campaign in Vietnam. He feared the United States could not accomplish its political goals through the application of military force. Although McNamara supported the war in public, in private he was skeptical the United States would prevail. By summer 1967, McNamara and Undersecretary of State Nicholas Katzenbach were convinced the United States could not win in Vietnam at acceptable costs and should seek a negotiated settlement.[84] Much of their thinking was influenced by National Intelligence Estimates and CIA reports, such as the JASON Study, which suggested that U.S. bombing raids failed to diminish Hanoi's will to fight.[85] Appearing in August 1967 before a special Senate subcommittee investigating the air war, McNamara testified the bombings were not having the desired result. He warned the senators that "the air war in the North was no substitute for the ground war in the South, that bombing would not allow us to win on the cheap."[86]

In early November 1967, McNamara further distanced himself from the war by sending Johnson a memorandum that argued for a U.S. withdrawal.[87] McNamara urged the president to rethink the U.S. commitment to Vietnam: "Continuation of our present course in Southeast Asia would be dangerous, costly in lives, and unsatisfactory to the American people."[88] Unknown to McNamara at the time, Johnson had ordered CIA Director Richard Helms to investigate what would happen to U.S. credibility abroad if the United States withdrew from Vietnam. In a September 1967 report, seen only by the president and his national security adviser, Walt Rostow, Helms and his CIA analysts reported that "if the United States accepts failure in Vietnam, it will pay some price in the form of new risks which success there would preclude." But they also concluded, "The risks are probably more limited and controllable than most previous argument has indicated."[89] Johnson ignored Helms's report and fired McNamara, and the war raged on for another eight years. In the end, it would appear Helms and McNamara were correct.

It is interesting to note that despite his strong misgivings about the war and his very public stance against its escalation in 1967, McNamara came to symbolize all that was wrong in Vietnam. In the Kennedy years, many congressional critics found McNamara arrogant, too sure of himself and his policies. After 1965, when the conflict in Vietnam escalated into an American war, McNamara was the Johnson administration's key architect and policy spokesman. He constantly briefed Congress and the American public on the significant progress being made in the war, and he warned detractors they would be on the losing side of history. He delivered this message with a sureness that made many in Washington nervous. His personal style turned many supporters against the war, and his insistence the administration was on the right track in Vietnam only underscored the growing congressional doubts about success there. When the military began to have misgivings about the limited-war strategy in Vietnam, McNamara became the focus of their ire. He was an easy, even if undeserving, target for their frustrations.

Forty years later, Secretary of Defense Donald Rumsfeld likewise finds himself overidentified with the war in Iraq and its failures. Once again, military leaders are questioning the leadership capabilities of the secretary of defense. Rumsfeld's insistence that the United States is on the right track in Iraq despite evidence to the contrary has prompted many former military leaders, including generals with leadership experience there, to call for his resignation. The encore is that a secretary of defense is justifying a losing proposition with arrogant statements about U.S. objectives and success. From his first days at the Pentagon, many of Rumsfeld's detractors have pointed to a similarity in personality and style between Rumsfeld and McNamara. Former Secretary of Defense Melvin Laird has described Rumsfeld as having an "overconfident and self-assured style on every issue," and that has turned many in Congress and the military against the administration.[90] In both wars, then, the secretary of defense became the flash point for military aggravation.

Several members of Congress fear that the Bush administration is repeating many of the Johnson administration's mistakes and that Rumsfeld, indeed, is doing his best to impersonate McNamara. At the core of the problem, in their view, is the idea that U.S. credibility is again at stake.[91] As in Vietnam, critics of the war in Iraq say the administration, especially Rumsfeld, is not being realistic about the consequences of a U.S. withdrawal. Only one major European ally has joined the "coalition of the willing"—Great Britain—and other allies, such as Spain and Italy, have withdrawn their troops altogether. The Bush administration counters that there has not been another attack on American soil since the invasion of Iraq, and that troops will not be withdrawn until the job is done. Furthermore, supporters of the war believe, a U.S. withdrawal before the coalition government can stand on its own will tell the terrorists that their goal of creating more theocratic states can be achieved simply by shedding American blood. Credibility is therefore the focal point of both wars.

CONSEQUENCES OF WITHDRAWAL

In Iraq, as in Vietnam, talk of a U.S. withdrawal stokes fears of a subsequent bloodbath. The Bush administration rightfully worries that premature withdrawal from Iraq will precipitate a chaotic and bloody civil war there. The president seems determined to stay the course to avoid such a fate, even if this means extending the U.S. commitment beyond the public's willingness to support such a measure. Growing sectarian violence in Iraq threatens the Bush administration's fragile domestic coalition on Iraq, and U.S. public opinion polls highlight growing support for a U.S. withdrawal.[92] Many observers in Washington see no easy way out.

On the one hand, if the Bush administration stays too long in Iraq, American citizens will grow weary and press their representatives to alter U.S. foreign policy fundamentally, as occurred following the Vietnam War. An "Iraq Syndrome" will join the "Vietnam Syndrome" in dominating all foreign-policy discussions. If, on the other hand, the Bush administration pulls out of Iraq before it can stand on its own against the insurgents, that same public will no doubt compare Bush's policy to that of Nixon's "decent interval."

Throughout 1971 and 1972, Nixon and his national security adviser, Henry Kissinger, made it clear to Hanoi and its allies in Moscow and Beijing that the United States was willing to strike a deal to end the war following the November 1972 U.S. presidential elections. Kissinger secretly met with Chinese Premier Zhou En-lai in Beijing on July 9, 1971, in preparation for Nixon's 1972 visit. Kissinger told Zhou the United States would exchange its complete withdrawal of U.S. troops for the return of American POWs and a cease-fire throughout all of Indochina. Kissinger declared that Nixon thereafter would need a guarantee there would be an interval—described variously as "a reasonable interval," "a sufficient interval," "a decent interval"—between the cease-fire and a resumption of hostilities between North and South Vietnam.[93] In a follow-up meeting, he pressed his Chinese host on the timing of such hostilities, arguing they could not resume immediately. "All we ask," Kissinger concluded, "is a degree of time so as to leave Vietnam for Americans in a better perspective."[94] If a month after a U.S. withdrawal "the war starts again, it is quite possible we would say this was just a trick to get us out and we cannot accept this. If the North Vietnamese, on the other hand, engage in a serious negotiation with the South Vietnamese, and if after a longer period it starts again after we are all disengaged . . . it is much less likely that we will go back [to Vietnam] again."[95]

The skillful Zhou pressed Kissinger to clarify his meaning. The Chinese wanted an end to the Vietnam war too and were perfectly willing to trade on Hanoi's wishes for better relations with the United States. Zhou wanted to see how far Kissinger was willing to go toward peace. Zhou asked, "So the outcome of your logic is that the war will continue?" Kissinger replied, "Why should we be afraid of socialism in Vietnam when we can live with communism in China?"[96] That was all Zhou needed to hear. The Nixon administration was pursuing a dual track in Vietnam. The first track was to continue to apply military pressure on Hanoi through the mining of Haiphong harbor, increased bombing raids against North Vietnam, and U.S. military incursions into Laos and Cambodia designed to break up Communist supply routes and sanctuaries. The second track, and the more likely scenario, was the "decent interval." The United States would withdraw its troops completely in exchange for American POWs and a guarantee that a reasonable time would pass between the U.S. pullout and the resumption of hostilities. But how long was enough?

Nixon believed the timing of the decent interval was crucial to his foreign-policy goals. He supported Kissinger's stance in China, and in fact had endorsed it in several White House meetings with his national security adviser. He pressed Kissinger, however, on the long-term consequences. Nixon wondered if the anticipated North Vietnamese defeat of South Vietnam would cost his administration too much and if Kissinger could guarantee a decent interval. The president asked how the United States could gain control of events in Vietnam without troops on the ground.[97] Kissinger answered, "If a year or two years from now North Vietnam gobbles up South Vietnam, we can have a viable foreign policy if it looks as if it's the result of South Vietnamese incompetence."[98]

The president liked the plan, as long as it coalesced after the 1972 U.S. election. When South Vietnamese President Nguyen van Thieu realized what Kissinger and Nixon had in mind, he wept openly. The Nixon administration would eventually ask South Vietnam to sign an agreement that forced a U.S. withdrawal, released U.S. prisoners of war, and provided no military or political guarantee for the security and longevity of South Vietnam. South Vietnam was being forced to commit suicide. However, Nixon and Kissinger had done their homework. They recognized there was little support in the United States for prolonging the war after the election the Saigon government called for in 1971. More important, after that the Saigon government lost the faith of a majority of the American people.

In that election, President Thieu won by a landslide, primarily by disqualifying his political opponents. The Nixon administration had pressed the Thieu government to hold new elections from early 1969 on. A reluctant Thieu eventually agreed to the proposal, and elections were scheduled for October 1971. Thieu had narrowly won favor in 1967, and he feared any new election carried with it the potential to oust his government. The economy was in a shambles, the Communists had made huge advances since the beginning of the phased U.S. withdrawal, and public support for the war inside South Vietnam was diminishing rapidly. Furthermore, Thieu understood the American public was growing tired of supporting the war in Vietnam. Still, Thieu could not bear the possibility that he might lose an open election. Accordingly, he did everything in his power—which was considerable—to ensure that no serious challenge was made to his rule.

The Nixon administration was outraged by Thieu's behavior. During negotiations in Paris, the Communist Party's chief diplomat, Le Duc Tho, suggested to Kissinger that the United States could withdraw from Vietnam under the cover of elections if Washington worked hard to guarantee that all qualified candidates were in the pool.[99] According to Tho, Thieu would lose any national election that included candidates who would be willing to negotiate a cease-fire and settlement with the National Liberation Front.[100] Therefore, Tho reasoned, the United States could claim Thieu had been deposed legally, and Hanoi would have a legitimate shot at regime change in Saigon. From the time the Paris negotiations had been made public, it was Hanoi's official policy to insist that the United States stop offering its unconditional support to Thieu. The Communists believed they could take South Vietnam through the moral superiority of their political program if only they were allowed a reasonable chance in national elections. The Nixon administration had rejected this call during its first two years, but by 1971 there was some support for an open election in Saigon.

Despite the Nixon administration's efforts to force Thieu into a truly democratic election, the South Vietnamese president managed to keep the election a one-man race. Early in 1971, Thieu learned that

South Vietnam's vice president, Nguyen Cao Ky, was interested in running for the nation's highest office. Thieu used a technicality in a newly approved election law to disqualify Ky. General Duong van Minh (known in the West as Big Minh) also wanted to run. Minh was on record as approving open negotiations with some NLF leaders, although he stopped short of endorsing a fully negotiated settlement. After Thieu had eliminated Ky's candidacy, the U.S. embassy in Saigon supported General Minh's presidential aspirations. Apparently, U.S. Ambassador Ellsworth Bunker tried to bribe Minh to run in order to make the election look "more democratic."[101] In the end, Thieu was the only candidate for the office of president of South Vietnam. He used funds from the CIA to win reelection by a landslide by buying votes. The Nixon administration learned it could not count on democratic elections in South Vietnam to bring peace or to precipitate a U.S. withdrawal.

Today in Iraq there are similar fears. Many Americans are growing weary of the way the new government in Baghdad is running its affairs. For example, in early February 2006, the newly elected Baghdad government announced it was nominating Prime Minister Ibrahim al-Jaafari for a second term. For most foreign observers, however, al-Jaafari's nomination did not come as welcome news. He did little in his first term to stem the torture and indiscriminate arrests in Sunni neighborhoods, and many of the economic programs he supported were an unmitigated disaster. Many Sunnis in Iraq also fear al-Jaafari owes his position to a deal struck with followers of Muqtada al-Sadr and his Mahdi Army. Support from al-Sadr comes at a cost, and that cost might cause many Americans to turn their backs on the nation-building experiment in Iraq. Clearly, al-Sadr and his followers, who control many of the Shiite neighborhoods in

Baghdad and Basra, want a Taliban-style government in Iraq and closer ties with U.S. enemies in Iran and Syria. Since the nomination, attacks against U.S. troops by the Mahdi Army have increased dramatically. If Iraqi elections produce such chaos, many Americans will lose faith and demand a U.S. withdrawal, just as they did in Vietnam. Under enormous political pressure, Baghdad eventually withdrew al-Jaafari's nomination in April 2006. However, the proposed coalition in the new prime minister's office will also face an uphill struggle trying to unite the people of Iraq.

THE HIGH COST OF WAR

Another major concern for Americans is the growing cost of the war in Iraq. Despite looming deficits, a lackluster domestic economy, and unexpected expenses attributed to Hurricane Katrina and other natural disasters, policymakers in Washington have spent an average of $6.8 billion per month in Iraq since the April 2003 invasion. Congress has approved another $50 billion for fiscal year 2006, which began October 1, 2005. Many Americans think this money would be better spent in other ways, and the Bush administration will find it increasingly difficult to continue to ask Congress for additional funds for the war if Baghdad doesn't show more progress and the U.S. economy doesn't improve. Eventually, the president may find himself facing the same conundrum that haunted Lyndon Johnson: how to pay for an unpopular war?

For Johnson, the answer came in the form of a war surtax. Convinced he needed to continue to fund his Great Society social programs and the war in Vietnam, Johnson reluctantly introduced a special personal income tax in January 1968. Within three months, he

expanded that tax to include business profits. Johnson announced the
10 percent surtax shortly before the Tet offensive, making the American public all the more skeptical of his plans. Johnson had rejected
such measures throughout the first three years of his presidency, but
by late 1967 it was clear he had no choice but to raise taxes to pay for
the war's growing costs.

Old "cold warriors" Dean Acheson, Paul Nitze, and W. Averell
Harriman believed the United States faced a serious financial crisis if
it could not control the war's costs. For these three giants of the cold
war, that crisis had the potential to be far more damaging to U.S.
security interests than would the loss of South Vietnam to Ho Chi
Minh. They urged Johnson to rethink U.S. policy in Vietnam and to
get a handle on costs. Adding to Johnson's troubles was a major melt-
down in the British economy, causing a significant drop in value of
the British pound sterling. The fallout of this was that U.S. gold
slipped in value, losing over $370 million in trading during a single
day.[102] According to Dean Acheson, Harry Truman's secretary of
state, the gold crisis dampened "expansionist ideas" in Washington,
forcing the president to reject Westmoreland's new troop-increase
request in early 1968.[103]

Financial crisis and declining public support for the war following
Tet forced Johnson from office. On March 31, 1968, the president
announced he would not seek and would not accept his party's nomination for the 1968 presidential election. A dejected Johnson spent
his remaining months in office desperately seeking an end to the war
in Vietnam and full funding for his Great Society programs. He got
neither. Instead, Johnson presided over the origins of the first sustained U.S. economic recession, which would last from 1968 until the
early 1980s. This economic downturn represented the first time since

World War II that the U.S. economy did not rebound. Economic growth so characteristic of the early cold-war years gave way to massive deficits, trade imbalances, and new regressive taxes. In the end, Lyndon Johnson found it impossible to maintain public support for both his war and his social programs. He could not have guns and butter.

Although the Bush administration does not face the same election-year crisis as Lyndon Johnson, most Americans clearly believe there is a limit to how much the United States can spend in Iraq. At a time when the president favors tax cuts, doubt is growing in some Washington circles that the administration can have it all. In the end, it is likely the Bush administration will withdraw from Iraq because of public pressure. Although the Republican-controlled Congress is unlikely to pass a resolution demanding a troop withdrawal, the president probably will respond to growing public discord. Increasing American casualties, setbacks in nation building, and rising war costs will influence all future discussions on Iraq.

Perhaps the most important issue, however, is the continued sectarian violence there. After the substantial U.S. investment in Iraq, the American people are unlikely to continue supporting the war if Iraq does not find a way to govern legitimately. In early 2006, the U.S. ambassador to Iraq, Zalmay Khalilzad, hinted the Bush administration could not continue to pump billions of dollars in U.S. economic aid into Iraq if the violence between Sunnis and Shiites continued. Particularly disturbing to the ambassador were growing reports that the NIA and the police force had instigated some of the attacks. Khalilzad has tried to coax moderate Sunni leaders into the coalition government and away from radical elements of the insurgency, knowing full well that time is not on his side. New attacks against Shiite holy sites in February 2006 suggest that his efforts are not paying off. For Khalilzad, Iraq is taking on Vietnam-like qualities because there is mounting public pressure for results when the momentum is all in the other direction. Americans do not have much patience for inconclusive conflicts. This is a lesson the Bush administration should have learned from Vietnam before it invaded Iraq in March 2003.

THE WAR AT HOME

The Bush White House has been fortunate that the American public is registering its disapproval of the war primarily through public opinion polls and its representatives in Congress. Unlike the Johnson and Nixon administrations, President Bush has been spared massive antiwar protests. During the Vietnam War, hundreds of thousands of protesters took to the streets. Perhaps the most significant protests were the massive national moratoriums against the war held in Washington, D.C. In October 1967, antiwar protesters gathered in Washington for seven days of speeches, songs, and marches. The most dramatic demonstration came on October 21, 1967, with a march against the Pentagon. As many as 35,000 protesters walked from the Lincoln Memorial across the Potomac River to the "nerve center of the war."[104] They formed a human chain around the Pentagon, trying to levitate it and exorcise its evil spirits. Many protesters tried to convince soldiers protecting the building to leave their posts. Toward the end of the evening, a serious clash broke out between antiwar activists and federal marshals who had been called in to keep the peace.

Two years later, protesters staged another march on Washington in November, which brought nearly one million people to the nation's capital. The protest was part of a larger strike against the war organized by the National Mobilization Committee to End the War in Vietnam (MOBE). In mid-October, MOBE had organized demonstrations in over fifty U.S. cities. Crowds of over 100,000 gathered in Boston, San Francisco, Philadelphia, and New York. With this success, MOBE joined forces with other antiwar groups to launch the national moratorium for November. Unlike the first march on Washington, however, the 1969 national moratorium featured middle-class Americans and gold-star mothers opposed to the war. They read the names of the American dead and placed placards bearing these names in coffins positioned outside the gates of the White House. Many mothers carried names of the sons they had lost in the war. In many ways, the protest movement had matured. This dramatic shift had a profound impact on public opinion. Throughout the early years of protest, many Americans found the radical elements of the antiwar movement more unsettling than the war itself. By 1969, however, the antiwar movement had gained momentum in middle-class homes and communities.

Returning Vietnam veterans also began to speak out against the war, making it more difficult for Nixon to continue to escalate the conflict. In one dramatic protest in April 1971, now known as Dewey Canyon III, Vietnam veterans returned their medals to Congress after making angry speeches about the war. During that protest, a young John Kerry appeared before the Senate Foreign Relations Committee, asking, "How do you ask a man to be the last man to die for a mistake?" Kerry was a member of a group called Vietnam Veterans Against the War (VVAW), an organization that had considerable influence in some middle-class communities.

Although growing numbers of Iraq veterans are organizing

against the war, their numbers are small compared with what VVAW mounted. Cindy Sheehan's protest at the Bush ranch over her son's death and the war in Iraq does not yet mirror a larger trend. The Bush administration has been spared the volatility of the 1960s and 1970s, but the American public clearly is growing war-weary. Furthermore, a number of retired U.S. generals have been openly critical of Secretary Rumsfeld and the plans for Iraq following Saddam Hussein's ouster. In many important ways, the protest against the war in Iraq—as limited as it is—might be as powerful as was the protest against the Vietnam War. Gold-star mothers and army generals have a way of grabbing the public's attention, and it will be difficult for the Bush administration to ignore these important, rational voices of protest.

CHAPTER FIVE

CHALLENGES TO
AMERICA'S POWER

D ESPITE the subtle similarities and the not-so-subtle differences between the Iraq and Vietnam wars, the most important parallel is the challenge each conflict has presented to American power. In Vietnam, the United States learned that power had limits. Key members of the Kennedy and Johnson administrations believed they could channel radical revolution along liberal lines through economic development and political reform. They argued they could halt the inevitable path of history and redirect it toward liberal democracy through will and force. Neoconservatives in the administration during George W. Bush's first term had a similar argument. They also believed they could export democracy and this alone would transform terrorists into democrats. Never mind that most of the terrorists had experience with democracy in Europe and were radicalized within democracy's borders. The neoconservatives argued that "history could be pushed along with the right application of power and will."[1] All these voices were equally wrong. The most striking similarity between Iraq and Vietnam, then, is the shared illusion about the efficacy and limitlessness of U.S. power.

In each war, U.S. political leaders believed in the old Wilsonian adage that spreading democracy abroad would make America and the world more secure. In Vietnam, the initial goal was not simply to stop the Communists but also to build a non-Communist alternative in South Vietnam. In Iraq, the central goal was regime change. The Bush administration believed it could take down Saddam Hussein and replace him with a democratic government. This would be the first step in promoting democracy throughout the region. Idealism and nobility of purpose, then, drove the United States to intervene in Vietnam and Iraq. Inside this idealism, however, was also the belief that the United States knew no limits to its power. American policy-makers believed in each case that regulating the world's political problems was not only desirable but also possible given U.S. power and will. Lyndon Johnson was fond of saying the mantle of freedom fell to the United States because no other country had the power to lift it. George W. Bush also believed the United States was the only nation that could defend freedom in the Middle East with power and conviction.

In Vietnam, though, the United States discovered there were indeed limits to what it could do by sheer will. Despite overwhelming force, technological superiority, and abundant financial resources, the United States was fundamentally incapable of coping with the enormous political complexities that inevitably emerge from a protracted military conflict. The policies of the "can-doers" Lyndon Johnson surrounded himself with did not do much to alter events in Vietnam. The United States spent over $167 billion in Vietnam but had very little to show for it. "The high hopes and wishful idealism with which the American nation had been born had not been destroyed" in Vietnam, a reporter for *Newsweek* observed, "but they had been chastened by the failure of America to work its will in Indochina."[2] Indeed, defeat in Vietnam caused a great crisis of will among those Americans who had once believed in the boundlessness of the nation's idealism. According to historian George Herring, Vietnam, like no other event in the nation's history, "challenged Americans' traditional beliefs about themselves, the notion that in their relations with other people they have generally acted with benevolence, the idea that nothing was beyond reach."[3]

Americans turned inward following Vietnam, fearful of any military engagements outside the defense of the continental United States, Alaska, and Hawaii. Polls taken in April 1975, just before the Communists captured Saigon, indicated only 36 percent of the American people felt the United States should keep its commitments to other nations, and a mere 34 percent expressed a willingness to defend West Berlin should the Soviets try to take it by force. According to some polls, a majority of Americans would not rescue any country—other than Canada—from military attack if they were commander in chief.[4] For several years, then, the United States withdrew from international politics. For example, from the beginning of the Korean War in 1950 to the end of the Vietnam War in 1975, over 100,000 American soldiers lost their lives in combat. From 1975 until 2000, another twenty-five-year period, fewer than 5,000 U.S. troops died in combat. Vietnam had indeed soured the nation on military intervention. Furthermore, the Vietnam War created a mood of despair in the United States. No one wanted to talk about the war, and political leaders did not want to repeat it. It was impossible to put Vietnam to rest, however, and soon people were talking about a

"Vietnam syndrome": an unwillingness to engage the world out of fear of another Vietnam.

THE VIETNAM SYNDROME

The syndrome began even before the war ended. On April 22, 1975, President Gerald Ford told an audience at Tulane University that the Vietnam War was "finished as far as the United States was concerned."[5] One week later, on April 30, 1975, Saigon fell to combined PAVN and PLAF forces, and the U.S. war in Vietnam was indeed over. Hanoi moved quickly to consolidate power and unite Vietnam under the socialist banner. In Washington, the White House blamed Congress for refusing a request for $722 million in emergency military assistance for South Vietnam. Ford and his secretary of state, Henry Kissinger, argued that additional aid might bring about the stalemate that all had hoped for in Vietnam, leading to a negotiated settlement between North and South Vietnam instead of an all-out Communist victory. Kissinger publicly worried that "pulling the plug" on South Vietnam would have dire consequences for U.S. prestige in the world and that it would doom the South Vietnamese to "lingering deaths."[6] Congress, in sharp contrast, claimed RVNAF troops had abandoned more military equipment in late 1974 and early 1975 than all the emergency aid could buy. Published photographs of RVNAF soldiers fleeing Phuoc Long, Hue, and Da Nang ahead of the Communists did not endear Congress to Saigon's cause. It was time, Congress declared, to end U.S. involvement in this "horrid war."[7]

After the fall of Saigon, U.S. policymakers dealt with the Vietnam syndrome in a variety of ways. Some, like Henry Kissinger, argued the United States needed to abandon the reckless liberalism of the early cold war and focus more on its realistic national interests. Shortly after the war, Kissinger concluded "we probably made a mistake" by focusing single-mindedly on international communism and falling dominos when dealing with Vietnam. "We perhaps might have perceived the war more in Vietnamese terms," he conceded, "rather than as the outward thrust of a global conspiracy."[8] In his view, the United States had stretched itself too thin in Vietnam and in the future must define its interests more narrowly. Like the European statesmen he had written about, Kissinger believed the true responsibility of a great power was in "knowing when to stop."[9] Kissinger recognized the United States could not fight a protracted war again and maintain its other, more vital interests. The Soviet Union had reached nuclear parity while the United States was bogged down in the jungles of Southeast Asia, and it had also greatly expanded its naval fleet. Both developments changed the power relationship between the superpower rivals, and this worried Kissinger more than the loss of South Vietnam.

Others tried to suggest America could have won the Vietnam War and the experience was no reason to limit U.S. global responsibilities. Nixon's secretary of defense, James Schlesinger, claimed the military had operated with too many restrictions. U.S. Army Colonel Harry Summers agreed, advising that in the future the United States needed to bring all-out military force to bear in any conflict. General William Westmoreland believed his attrition strategy could have worked in Vietnam if only the American people had not suffered a failure of will during the Tet offensive. Some advisers suggested the problem rested with U.S. allies in Saigon. Without a viable government and a strong national army, how could the United States have achieved victory? McGeorge Bundy, national security adviser for

Kennedy and Johnson, warned that Vietnam taught no useful lessons because the war was unique and probably not to be repeated. Americans, the Vietnam apologists all argued, should get over the war and turn their attention to the pressing international problems of the day.

But Congress still felt the limits to U.S. power following Vietnam. Six months after Saigon fell, Portugal granted its former colony, Angola, independence following a bloody civil war. The announcement set off another internal conflict involving the Soviet-supported Popular Movement for the Liberation of Angola (MPLA). The CIA spent $32 million on covert aid to the MPLA's rivals, hoping to control the revolution and events in Africa. The State Department official in charge of African affairs, Nathaniel Davis, urged the Ford administration to engage in trilateral diplomacy, bringing in neighboring Tanzania and Zambia to help negotiate a peaceful settlement. President Ford rejected Davis's advice, opting instead for more covert aid and a military solution. Davis resigned in protest and let several members of Congress know the Ford administration had rejected the diplomatic path. As the MPLA made headway against its adversaries, Ford prepared to ask Congress for an additional $25 million for arms and covert aid. Congress balked, voting down the proposal by a wide margin. Kissinger immediately complained that Americans were traumatized by Vietnam. Ford concluded that Vietnam had caused members of Congress to "lose their guts."[10]

The Carter administration also experienced the hangover effect from Vietnam. Carter came to office in 1977 promising to cut military budgets, reduce U.S. forces overseas, trim arms sales abroad, and support allies who followed his human rights agenda. He vowed there would be "no more Vietnams." Carter was deeply troubled by the malaise that had gripped the nation since Vietnam. He believed the

American people would no longer accept U.S. military intervention in faraway places for dubious reasons. He argued the United States could not "prop up a series of regimes that lacked popular support," and "there can be no going back to a time when we thought there could be American solutions to every problem."[11] Carter realized newly emerging postcolonial nations were in revolt because of grinding poverty, social and racial problems, and political difficulties, not international communism. He wanted to reorient U.S. relations with the developing world, erasing the "intellectual and moral poverty" of military intervention that had been demonstrated in Vietnam.[12]

Yet Carter was also a "cold warrior." He insisted détente had allowed the Soviets to increase their domination of Eastern Europe, and he was highly critical of grain sales to Moscow. He reinvigorated the containment doctrine by initiating new weapons systems and by cultivating friendly governments in the Southern Hemisphere. When the Soviet Union invaded Afghanistan in 1979, Carter launched a new phase of containment. He armed many of Moscow's neighbors, such as Pakistan, and created several new naval facilities in Oman, Kenya, Somalia, and Egypt. Carter also opened formal diplomatic relations with the People's Republic of China, a move he was sure would make the Soviets think twice about more aggressive action. In his State of the Union address of January 23, 1980, the president announced the Carter Doctrine: "An attempt by any outside force to gain control of the Persian Gulf region will be regarded as an assault on the vital interests of the United States of America, and such an assault will be repelled by use of any means necessary, including military force."[13] Carter even declared a U.S. boycott of the 1980 summer Olympics in Moscow to protest the Soviet invasion of Afghanistan.

Carter's bold words caused many in Washington to proclaim that the Vietnam syndrome was already cured. But others knew better. George F. Kennan, the father of the original containment policy, suggested Carter was long on words and short on action. He concluded the president was using "thundering" rhetoric but carrying "a very small stick."[14] Kennan knew what others knew. At the height of a devastating economic crisis at home, and in the shadow of Vietnam, Congress was not likely to approve of any bold plans that included direct military action against the Soviets. The United States could fight wars with proxies in the post-Vietnam era, but Congress would not go along with the full mobilization of U.S. troops to save Afghanistan—or any other nation in the region, for that matter. When Carter promised $400 million to Pakistan for its defense against a potential Soviet invasion, the Pakistani prime minister called it "peanuts."[15] Indeed, Carter was trying to fight the cold war with one hand tied behind his back. The knot was Vietnam. The hostage crisis in Iran in 1979 simply underscored Carter's inability to move the nation to a war footing so soon after the fall of Saigon.

Other signs indicated Carter and the country were still suffering from Vietnam syndrome. In 1975 the Khmer Rouge took over Cambodia following a brutal civil war against the U.S.-backed Lon Nol government. The Khmer Rouge were not only Maoists but perhaps even more fanatical about the moral superiority of their ideas. Once they seized power, the Communists emptied Phnom Penh and other Cambodian cities, creating a nation of refugees. They relocated the urban Cambodians to rural areas and forced them to work at meaningless tasks in death camps. Over time, the Khmer Rouge instituted one of the most reprehensible genocidal programs in history, killing over one-third of the entire Cambodian population. During this purge, the Carter administration sat on the sidelines. Of course, Washington's new relationship with Beijing made it difficult for the Carter administration to protest Khmer Rouge atrocities—China was the Khmer Rouge's major benefactor—but U.S. officials turned their backs fearing another Vietnam. Carter purposefully avoided the genocide in Cambodia, according to John Mueller, because of "fears that paying attention might lead to the conclusion that American troops should be sent over to rectify the disaster."[16] Carter was not alone in ignoring the problems in Cambodia. The three television networks devoted fewer than thirty minutes to coverage of the genocide that lasted over three years, and Congress failed to pass any resolutions condemning the Khmer Rouge and calling for united action.

Congress did go along with increased military budgets, however. If Carter could not deploy U.S. troops for fear of another Vietnam, he definitely intended to beef up the U.S. defense arsenal. The president deployed the MX intercontinental missile and added $47 billion in new weapons systems. The Pentagon's budget jumped from $170 billion in 1976 to $197 billion in 1981. Carter also doubled arms sales to U.S. allies between 1977 and 1980 to $15.3 billion.[17] Some critics suggested Carter was trying to "remilitarize" the United States, but others concluded he had been "too soft" on the Soviets and America's enemies.[18] His public opinion polls in the area of foreign affairs were some of the lowest of the twentieth century. Only 17 percent of Americans polled in 1980 gave the president a satisfactory rating.[19] For many Americans, Carter's mixed foreign-policy agenda reinforced their desire to isolate themselves from the rest of the world. In retrospect, Carter's problem was that he did not want to get involved in another Vietnam-type conflict, but the world held only more of the same. Afghanistan promised no easy solutions, and the civil wars in Central America were also open-ended commitments. Given the reluctance of Congress and the American people to repeat the Vietnam experience, the only avenue available to the president other than military intervention was to build up America's deterrent capabilities.

Carter could never balance U.S. fear of "more Vietnams" with broader foreign-policy objectives. His opponent in the 1980 presidential election found a solution to this foreign-relations dilemma through tough cold-war rhetoric that denied Vietnam was a defeat. Candidate Ronald Reagan claimed policymakers in Washington had gotten Vietnam all wrong. "For far too long," Reagan declared in August 1980, "we have lived with the Vietnam Syndrome. This is a lesson for all of us in Vietnam. If we are forced to fight, we must have the means and the determination to prevail, or we will not have what it takes to secure peace. And while we are at it, let us tell those who fought in that war that we will never again ask young men to fight and possibly die in a war our government is afraid to let them win."[20] Reagan was hoping to revise America's understanding of Vietnam and its meanings in order to pursue a more aggressive foreign-policy agenda. Carter's military-budget increases paved the way for the Reagan administration to fight the cold war using new weapons and covert CIA operations.

THE WEINBERGER DOCTRINE

Despite Reagan's expansive rhetoric and expanded military budgets, however, his administration was the first after Vietnam to put parameters on U.S. military operations. In a speech before the National Press Club in November 1984, Reagan's secretary of defense, Caspar

Weinberger, announced the administration's new defense posture following the 1983 bombing of a U.S. Marine barracks at the Beirut airport in Lebanon. That stunning terrorist act had caused the Reagan administration to withdraw all troops from Lebanon. The president did not want to isolate the United States from other overseas actions, but he did want the Defense Department to prepare a plan summarizing the lessons learned from Beirut and Vietnam. These lessons were distilled into six major points that became known as the Weinberger Doctrine:

1. The United States should not commit forces to combat unless the vital national interests of the United States or its allies are involved.
2. U.S. troops should only be committed wholeheartedly and with the clear intention of winning. Otherwise, troops should not be committed.
3. U.S. combat troops should be committed to conflicts with clearly defined political and military objectives and with the capacity to accomplish those objectives.
4. The relationship between the objectives and the force structure should be continually reassessed and adjusted if necessary.
5. U.S. troops should be committed only when there is reasonable assurance that Congress and the American people will support the action.
6. The use of arms should be the last resort to protect U.S. interests.

After the attack in Beirut and against the backdrop of Vietnam, Weinberger was limiting where and when the United States would engage in military intervention. Reagan's secretary of state, George Shultz, was a staunch critic of the Weinberger Doctrine, arguing that diplomacy needed the constant threat of military force to succeed. Shultz did not believe the nation was suffering from any Vietnam syndrome, and he thought Congress would support U.S. military intervention whenever and wherever it was needed.

Given these parameters, the Reagan administration never asked the American people to make painful sacrifices to support its foreign-policy agenda. Despite military intervention in several Central American countries, Reagan and Weinberger managed to keep U.S. military action quite limited on their watch. Few U.S. soldiers died in combat during the Reagan years, and there was no full-scale mobilization of the armed forces. Despite claims from many quarters that U.S. intervention in Nicaragua and El Salvador signaled new Vietnams, those conflicts resolved themselves in ways that proved critics wrong. Reagan did not use the U.S. military to destabilize unfriendly regimes or to support friendly ones; instead he used covert aid, CIA operations, and economic incentives to influence politics in the region. In Nicaragua and El Salvador, Reagan's support of authoritarian governments came more in the form of aid to proxy armies than in direct U.S. military intervention. Even the administration's support of the contras in Nicaragua was limited militarily. The CIA helped the contras mine three Nicaraguan ports and built large bases in neighboring Honduras, but there was no full-scale use of U.S. forces against the Sandinistas.

The combination of the Beirut bombing and the legacy of Vietnam indeed limited the president's use of force in undefined struggles. Instead of military intervention, the Reagan administration used America's unchallenged economic resources to confront internal and external threats. The president increased military spending by 40 percent between 1980 and 1984 while cutting taxes. He believed he could outspend and outarm the Soviets with beneficial results. Reagan's flirtations with the Strategic Defense Initiative (SDI) were an outgrowth of that thinking. This missile shield was short on science but long on cost, and the administration believed it would force the Soviets into even more expensive weapon systems that did not significantly alter the strategic balance. The collapse of the Soviet Union was one sure sign that Reagan's policy of limiting U.S. military action abroad and focusing on a spiraling arms race had worked. However, that policy left the United States with record budget deficits, nearly $1 trillion, and a soaring balance-of-trade deficit. Still, most Americans felt confident about the nation's place in the world, and few feared the United States would be engaged in another Vietnam so soon after the collapse of South Vietnam.

THE POWELL DOCTRINE

After Reagan left office, many of his administration's views on military intervention survived with Colin Powell. Powell, a Vietnam veteran and a disciple of Caspar Weinberger, maintained the United States must continue to use its economic power, diplomatic skills, and multilateral support as the cornerstones of all foreign-policy actions. He warned that the United States should never lead with armed forces. He said the country had to ask itself a series of questions before it actively engaged in military conflict:

1. Is the political objective we seek to achieve important?
2. Does it have a clearly defined objective that is easily understood?

3. Have all other nonviolent policy means failed?

4. Will military force achieve the objective?

5. At what cost can the objective be reached?

6. Have the gains and risks been analyzed?

7. How might the situation that we seek to alter, once it is altered by force, develop further and what might be the consequences?

In short, the Powell Doctrine brought Weinberger's thinking into the 1990s.

Powell also outlined the military's willingness in the post-Vietnam era to ask hard questions and to make fundamental changes to its culture. Rejecting much of the academic thinking that held sway during the cold war, the services returned to the basics. One of the first significant changes was the introduction of courses on strategy in the service academies.[21] These courses emphasized history over academic theory. Students studied the classic battles and investigated writers long ignored. Sun Tzu and Carl von Clausewitz became familiar names at West Point and Annapolis once again. Along with this renewed emphasis on military history and strategy came a belief among the officers that Vietnam's principal lesson was the United States should never again find itself in that position. The military began to concentrate again on the Soviet threat in Europe and to prepare for a more conventional war on the Continent. Officers also came to reject many of the theories of protracted and limited war as applied in Vietnam. Instead, those with Vietnam experience insisted there were limits to U.S. power. They told their troops there was not always a military solution to complex political problems.

Another significant development to ensure no more Vietnams

was the move to make sure service reserve troops were completely integrated into any mobilization scheme. During the Vietnam War, President Johnson refused McNamara's request to mobilize the reserves in 1965, fearing the American public would see such a move as a sure sign the war would require enormous sacrifice. Furthermore, Johnson wanted to limit public debate by fighting the war in cold blood. He worried that mobilizing the reserves might spark a heated debate in Congress. Accordingly, when Johnson introduced combat troops for the first time in March 1965, the reserves stayed home. It did not take long, however, for officers to complain to their commanders that without the reserves, they presided over a depleted, unskilled, and demoralized army. The lack of reserves also meant that many jobs usually given to support troops went to regular army, putting further pressure on force structure. Even though Johnson routinely said he had given General Westmoreland everything he asked for, even abbreviated investigation would have revealed that officers in Vietnam rarely believed they had enough troops.

General Creighton Abrams, who served as U.S. Army chief of staff in the last years of the Vietnam War, negotiated a new look for the army with Secretary of Defense James Schlesinger. Abrams increased its size to sixteen divisions without increasing the number of regular forces above 785,000.[22] He did this by assigning most support functions to an expanded army reserve. The link with the regular army became so tight that Abrams guaranteed there could be no war without mobilizing the reserves. "They're not taking us to war again without calling up the reserves," Abrams was fond of saying.[23] The impact of this policy was felt immediately. Coupled with the Goldwater-Nichols Act of 1986, which gave the head of the Joint Chiefs of Staff greater responsibility over all service branches and allowed for coordinated and integrated training among the services, the new reserve-force structure meant the army would never be short of troops again. By the time of the first Gulf War, according to Herring, 70 percent of the army's support services, 60 percent of the air force's strategic airlift units, and 93 percent of the navy's cargo-handling battalions were with the reserves.[24] When the first President Bush took the nation to war in Iraq and Kuwait in 1991, he had no choice but to call up the reserves, and this arrangement made the president keep goals, objectives, and force structure in line.

Bush's mobilization for war followed Saddam Hussein's August 1990 invasion of Kuwait. After the Iraqi offensive into Kuwait, the Bush White House began making military plans for an air and ground offensive against Iraq should diplomacy fail. In late November, the Bush administration secured a UN resolution authorizing the use of force to expel the Iraqi army from Kuwait. In early January, Congress granted Bush the right to use force against the Iraqi army and to defend Saudi Arabia and Israel should Saddam Hussein launch attacks against them. The UN gave Baghdad a deadline of January 15, 1991, to withdraw from Kuwait, a time limit that Saddam Hussein ignored. Accordingly, on January 17, the allied attack against Iraqi installations began. General Norman Schwarzkopf coordinated U.S. military action, combining air and ground attacks against key targets inside Iraq and Kuwait. In just six short weeks, allied military action forced Saddam Hussein to beat a hasty retreat out of Kuwait and back to Baghdad. In the process, thousands of Iraqis were killed, and military equipment worth millions of dollars was destroyed. The use of overwhelming force ensured victory. President Bush, applauding the U.S.-led effort, proclaimed, "By God, we've kicked the Vietnam syndrome."[25]

No, the Bush administration had not kicked the Vietnam syndrome. Instead, it had adopted a military strategy because of it. By massing overwhelming force for a very limited military objective, the administration was responding to nearly two decades of hard thinking on what had gone wrong in Vietnam. The force structure was commensurate with the job at hand, and the counterattacks against Iraq had the full support of Congress and the American people. Furthermore, the Bush administration had a UN resolution authorizing the action and several allies that went to battle alongside U.S. troops. Much of the Bush strategy rested on General Powell's ideas on the use of military power. Bush did not march to Baghdad to force regime change. His administration, with the help of an international coalition, simply removed Saddam Hussein from Kuwait by force. In fact, the limited response to Iraq's aggressive action against Kuwait earned George H.W. Bush sharp criticism from many of those who would become his son's strongest supporters. They argued the United States should have marched to Baghdad and thrown Saddam Hussein out of power then.[26]

Powell disagreed with the critics. He prophetically warned that to allow the United States to march to Baghdad was to ask for trouble. He opposed any U.S. military activity beyond the carefully prescribed UN resolution authorizing the use of force to expel Iraq from Kuwait. To do more, Powell insisted, was too great a risk. He explained in 1992 that if the first Gulf War had not been limited, "the United States would be ruling Baghdad today—at unpardonable expense in terms of money, lives lost, and ruined regional relationships."[27] Powell also suggested no military commander wanted to send his troops into harm's way without the full support of the American people and Congress. A march against Baghdad would surely topple Saddam Hussein, but then what? Powell did not want the country bogged down in a long-term nation-building project simply because it wanted regime change in Iraq. Like many of his fellow military leaders with Vietnam experience, Powell was cautious in the use of force. When it was applied, he wanted to have clear outcomes in mind and to use overwhelming force. The United States withdrew from the Iraqi theater with its limited objective met and its military ready for its next assignment.

THE GHOSTS OF VIETNAM

During the 1990s Balkan crisis, the Bush administration contemplated using force. When asked by a reporter if the United States would send troops to keep the peace among Bosnians, Serbs, and Croats, the president responded: "Everyone has been reluctant, for very understandable reasons, to use force. There are a lot of voices out there in the United States today that say 'use force,' but they don't have the same responsibility for sending somebody else's son or somebody else's daughter into harm's way. And I do. I do not want to see the United States bogged down in any way into some guerrilla warfare—we lived through that."[28]

Indeed, the Bosnian Serbs understood the United States did not want to repeat Vietnam in the Balkans. Bosnian Serb leader Radovan Karadzic boldly proclaimed his forces could have their way in the Balkans because the United States was paralyzed. He boasted the United States would have to send in 2,000 marines to put down his forces, "then they have to send 10,000 more to save the 2,000 . . . this is the best way to have another Vietnam."[29] Another Serb leader claimed the Balkans would be "a new Vietnam" if the United States sent in ground troops. According to Samantha Power, an expert on human rights and U.S. foreign policy, "'Vietnam' became the ubiquitous shorthand for all that could go wrong in the Balkans if the United States became militarily engaged."[30]

The ghosts of Vietnam also hampered the Clinton administration. Instead of immediately intervening in the Bosnian conflict, President Bill Clinton publicly vowed the United States would not send ground troops there, even to stop genocide. As *New York Times* journalist Drummond Ayres reported in May 1993, there was an "abiding fear that the Balkans are another Vietnam, a deep-seated angst that tends to outweigh concern that another holocaust is in the making."[31] This same fear kept the United States from intervening to stop the genocide in Rwanda. Instead of military intervention around the world, Clinton hoped to "engage" nations as the movement toward globalization and democracy naturally transpired. Clinton and his advisers believed the president had to supervise this development by removing restrictions on trade and investment and the circulation of ideas. If this process could bind the nations of the world, the Clinton administration reasoned, the root causes of violence and interstate rivalry would fade away.[32] There would be no reason to repeat the mistakes of Vietnam because the fundamental underpinnings of conflict would have been destroyed. When the United States got bloodied in Somalia, Clinton quickly pulled the troops out and left that region of the world to fend for itself.

At the end of the 1990s, however, some foreign-policy analysts claimed the pressing international questions were no longer about fears of another Vietnam but instead about ethical dilemmas concerning military intervention to support human rights. They asked how and when the United States and the United Nations should intervene to stop major human rights violations and genocide. Others suggested the move toward capitalism and democracy was irreversible and that U.S. foreign policy should be aimed at helping that process along, not at seeking monsters to destroy.[33] Still, there was a growing feeling among many policy analysts that the Clinton administration was indeed suffering from Vietnam syndrome. Its inability to "pull the trigger" in Rwanda to stop the genocide was a by-product of its worldview. Clinton's team players, most of them Vietnam-generation men and women, were hesitant to get involved in a complex situation that had no easy answers and elusive objectives. According to Samantha Power, administration officials were reluctant to get bogged down again, even if the cause was just.[34]

A major problem with fighting the Vietnam War was that the United States suffered from the challenges to its power for two decades. Defeat in Vietnam created a lasting feeling among many policymakers that they must avoid future Vietnams at all costs. The tragedy of Vietnam is that the misuse of force there limited U.S. military action where it might have been required later. How does the nation intervene in a messy situation like the Balkans or Rwanda after Vietnam? The Clinton administration never found a satisfactory answer until it was too late for tens of thousands of innocent people. One great lesson of Vietnam is that the United States must use power wisely. Another is that trouble will find a nation of America's power and responsibility without the United States looking for it. At the end of a long day, intervening in Vietnam's civil war probably cost the United States many of its more important geopolitical objectives, including stopping intrastate violence and genocide.

NEOCONSERVATIVES REJECT
THE VIETNAM SYNDROME

When George W. Bush decided to run for the presidency in 2000, he was certainly aware of the problems the Vietnam shadow cast on the Clinton administration. During the campaign, Bush repeatedly voiced his concern about America's confused role in the world. He made traditional realist arguments about the limits to U.S. power, warning that the United States should not overextend its reach. He believed the Clinton administration had pursued bad policy in the Balkans and in Africa, even if it had been limited. In the now-famous debate with Vice President Al Gore, candidate Bush stated he did not believe U.S. troops should be used in lengthy nation-building exercises. The United States should use its power only when vital U.S. interests were at stake, Bush claimed. Taking a page out of classic realism, Bush pledged he would never follow the path of the reckless liberals who took the United States to war in Vietnam with no clear goal, no clear sense of purpose, and no plan to win.

Neoconservatives, who had helped elect Bush in 2000, were concerned, however, that the new president was acting too much like a "Henry Kissinger realist." Kissinger, they argued, had placed too much confidence in détente and too much stock in internationalism. He emphasized that after the cold war, nations were free "to pursue foreign policies based increasingly on their immediate national interest." Furthermore, Kissinger argued, a new world order would emerge "much as it did in past centuries from a reconciliation and balancing of competing national interests."[35] The neocons urged the new president not to adopt a narrow view of U.S. national interests, as Kissinger had, hoping to convince Bush to accept their foreign-policy agenda.[36]

Neoconservatives such as Paul Wolfowitz, William Kristol, and Lawrence Kaplan also were right-wing Wilsonians who wanted to promote democracy around the world to strengthen it at home, a view in keeping with Woodrow Wilson's philosophy. They disagreed with Wilson's internationalism, though, favoring instead U.S. unilateral action outside of an international framework. Neoconservatives believe that international institutions, such as the United Nations, limit the United States and keep it from achieving many of its foreign-policy goals. Instead, they suggest the United States has the legitimate right to pursue its own agenda because it exerts a benevolent hegemony. Shortly before the Iraq War, two leading neoconservatives, William Kristol and Robert Kagan, claimed the world would accept U.S. efforts to promote democracy because the United States was inherently good and perceived that way: "It is precisely because American foreign policy is infused with an unusually high degree of morality that other nations find they have less to fear from its otherwise daunting power."[37] Some neoconservatives, such as Max Boot, even suggested that a return to empire was neither unfeasible nor unrealistic. In his essay "The Case for an American Empire," Boot declared that the United States should provide troubled countries with enlightened administration, much as the British did during the Raj.[38]

After the terrorist attacks on September 11, President Bush pursued an aggressive policy against America's enemies in Afghanistan. On September 18, 2001, the UN Security Council passed a resolution demanding the Taliban in Afghanistan hand over Osama bin Laden and close terrorist training camps inside the country's borders. The Taliban refused, arguing that the United States and its allies in the

United Nations had no proof bin Laden was connected to the September 11 attacks and that he should have his day in an Islamic court. The response was immediate and executed within a multilateral framework based on a United Nations resolution. On October 7, 2001, U.S. and British bombers attacked the Taliban in Kabul, Afghanistan's capital, and Kandahar, another Taliban stronghold. Ground troops followed, and soon an international coalition of eighteen nations was involved in the war on terrorism, including Japan who for the first time since World War II participated in military combat on a global scale. By December 2001, most of the Taliban had been defeated or had retreated to the mountains outside Tora Bora, the site of one of the last military engagements involving the Taliban, the terrorists, and the international coalition. Although remnants of the Taliban and the al-Qaeda terrorist network continue to harass coalition troops, the Bush administration struck a blow against terrorism with its swift and overwhelming response in Afghanistan.

In many ways, the attacks in Afghanistan followed the Powell Doctrine and the lessons of the Vietnam experience. The United States went to the UN for a Security Council resolution justifying the attacks inside an international framework. International support for the attacks was overwhelming, and public opinion around the world supported the United States in its hour of need. Perhaps at no time since the end of World War II had the nation enjoyed so much of the world's empathy. Bush used this international support wisely, building a coalition of willing allies to help the United States meet its limited objectives through the measured use of force. He also had the support of Congress, which passed a War Powers Resolution. It allowed President Bush to use the U.S. military against any force or any individual organization or state that was involved in the September 11 attacks or that sheltered, harbored, or assisted individuals involved in those attacks. Congress also passed a $40 billion appropriation bill to support the war on terrorism.

But something else happened in Afghanistan. Neoconservatives inside the Bush administration used the war on terror to push their larger agenda. They wanted to use U.S. power to promote democracy in the Middle East, and there is some evidence to suggest this planning was under way well before the September 11 attacks.[39] It now seems likely that the attacks on the United States by al-Qaeda convinced President Bush the neoconservatives were right. Perhaps it was time to use American might benevolently to create a new world order. Like many U.S. policymakers before him, President Bush believed the best defense against the terrorists was a good offense. The United States had the right to defend itself, the president claimed, but it also had a responsibility to make the world safe for democracy. As the world's only superpower, the United States had the power and the obligation to defend and promote democratic ideals. Leading neoconservatives William Kristol and Lawrence Kaplan agreed with the president, declaring the United States was in the driver's seat and should drive the car: "What is wrong with dominance in the service of sound principles and high ideals?"[40]

According to historian John Gaddis, the Bush administration's response to the events of September 11 was to "undertake the most fundamental reassessment of American grand strategy in over half a century."[41] Bush's new grand strategy embraced much of the neoconservatives' thinking on democracy promotion. Bush came to believe regime change was essential in Iraq, and promoting democracy through U.S. military power was the key to preventing future terrorist attacks. The United States had to extend peace through military intervention in a troubled region, according to the new thinking. This view separated the Bush administration from its predecessors. Although President Reagan talked of tearing down walls and promoting democracy, he rarely involved U.S. troops. George H.W. Bush used the military for a very limited objective and purposefully ruled out regime change and democracy promotion through force. President Clinton believed peace would happen naturally, without using the powerful U.S. military at all.

A NEW GRAND STRATEGY

George W. Bush's new grand strategy set out a policy line that denied Vietnam had happened at all. Ironically, just as in Vietnam, the United States would use its considerable power to influence events in a country far away and for a people it knew little about because key policymakers in Washington believed such a policy would make Americans safer. Promoting democracy or anticommunism promised to rid the world of the conditions that had created threats to American ideals. The appeal to ideals is what separates the George W. Bush administration from other post-Vietnam administrations. Other presidents talked about ideals, but few built military intervention around them. Policymakers did indeed restrict the use of military force to solve complex political problems in the post-Vietnam era. In the Balkans, President Clinton wanted to act early in the crisis but ultimately could not because he feared a long, drawn-out affair like Vietnam. But President Bush wanted to take the country on the offensive. The president's speech at West Point's graduation ceremonies in 2002 included these telling words: "We must take the battle to the enemy. . . . In the world we have entered the only path to safety is the path of action." Bush was clear about his moral certainty: "Moral truth is the same in every culture, in every time, and in every place. . . . We are in conflict between good and evil."[42] The appeal to American ideals did not go unnoticed by the cadets.

Shortly before the March 2003 invasion of Iraq, President Bush further distanced himself from the lessons of the Vietnam War by publicly proclaiming, "America's vital interests and our deepest beliefs are now one."[43] Attacking Iraq, the president claimed, was in U.S. national security interests, as was promoting democracy in the Middle East. Bush told the nation about U.S. war aims in clear and decisive language: "A liberated Iraq can show the power of freedom to transform that vital region. . . . Success in Iraq could also begin a new stage for Middle Eastern peace."[44] Wesley Clark, former commander of all coalition forces in Europe, worried the Bush administration's "quasi-imperial vision" would create an "army of empire." In his book *Winning Modern Wars,* Clark warned that the Bush administration sought a new world order based on aggressive policy goals built on the back of a powerful military: "This was to be a new America, reborn from adversity and threat, reaching out constructively to the world, liberating peoples, reforming a vital region, enabling the emergence of a new, universal morality, and taking advantage of this unique window of American military dominance to secure into the foreseeable future our security and safety."[45] For Clark and others, this vision was all too grand. It required too much of the military, and its hubris was overwhelming.

Since the U.S. mission in Iraq began to bog down in April 2004, democracy promotion has come under fierce attack at home from liberals and conservatives. Furthermore, the Bush administration's base of support for the mission appears to be drying up, in the same way liberals abandoned President Johnson. Conservative Americans from the "red states" supported the war in Iraq because they believed Saddam Hussein did have weapons of mass destruction and he was an important link in the international terrorist network. Now that the war in Iraq can be characterized instead as a nation-building experiment to promote democracy, former supporters of the war are turning against the administration. Even some neoconservatives no longer believe in the cause. Francis Fukuyama has rejected the notion that history can be pushed along by U.S. power and will.[46]

AN IRAQ SYNDROME?

Since the overthrow of Saddam Hussein, the Bush administration has had little success in Iraq. The new government is having difficulty convincing Sunnis they have a stake in the future of the country. Some Sunnis have protested that the national army and the police purposefully target them and their organizations. False arrests, torture, and confiscation of property are common complaints in Sunni communities. Sectarian violence also threatens to destroy the government. Insurgents have attacked Shiite holy sites, and reprisal attacks have left many ordinary Iraqis bloody. In addition, several key social and economic indicators of progress in Iraq point in the wrong direction. Unemployment and inflation remain huge problems, and the lack of reliable electricity and running water presents daily hurdles to a population already coping with tremendous stress. The number of civilian and U.S. casualties grows daily, as insurgents doubt that the United States has the staying power to finish the job in Iraq. To pay for the nation-building experiment, the Bush administration has had to return to Congress to ask for special appropriations. Congress so far has agreed, but the well will run dry eventually.

Some experts believe the best the Bush administration can hope for in Iraq is a "decent interval" akin to that pursued by the Nixon administration in Vietnam. They suggest Bush should create favorable conditions for the current government in Baghdad to assume full political responsibility for the nation and for the New Iraqi Army to take over security completely.[47] Once the handoff is complete, the United States should retreat as quickly as possible, though officials know a bloody civil war will likely break out in Iraq. The goal would be to have a decent interval between the U.S. withdrawal and total chaos. Supporters of this view are now in the minority, but their numbers increase with each passing day. It is difficult to see how the insurgency will be put down, how the sectarian violence will end, and how the nation will be reconstructed. The problems are huge, and their solutions do not appear imminent.

To many Americans, the United States seems to have come full circle. Once again it finds itself engaged in a war characterized by no clear boundaries, no clear exit strategy, no definition of victory, little allied support, no UN authority, growing public unrest, rising costs, and perhaps an inadequate number of troops for the job. Furthermore, suspicion is growing in Congress that the Bush administration did not exhaust all diplomatic avenues and that it never fully considered the consequences of U.S. military action against Iraq. Few officials in the Bush White House apparently ever contemplated what would follow Saddam Hussein and how difficult nation building would be. For many Americans, it appears as if the Bush administration learned nothing from the Vietnam War.

There is a new isolationism gripping America that resembles the withdrawal following Vietnam. A recent Pew Trust poll indicates a swing in public opinion away from internationalism and toward isolationism. According to some experts, the percentage of Americans who believe the United States "should mind its own business has never been higher since the end of the Vietnam war."[48] Will there be an "Iraq syndrome," one comparable to the Vietnam syndrome that forced the United States to take a hard look at its policies and practices? Will American policymakers place limits on U.S. power following the Iraq conflict as they did after Vietnam? Will this Iraq syndrome prevent a future president from using force when it is needed to stop a legitimate threat to U.S. national security or to protect humanitarian interests? The great parallel between Iraq and Vietnam is that the United States is indeed likely to slip into a post-Iraq syndrome that threatens America's use of power in the future. What America learned in Vietnam—and is now relearning in Iraq—is that there are indeed limits to U.S. power.

The neoconservatives who were the primary architects of the Iraq policy are now taking the blame for a policy gone wrong. The grand irony in Iraq is that the neocons' policy of promoting democracy through unilateral military action might actually have contributed to the defeat of their idealistic agenda. Not only has the public lost its taste for the war in Iraq, but the Bush administration also has made concerted efforts to distance itself from the neocons who promoted the war in the first place. Paul Wolfowitz has been kicked up to the World Bank, and the Bush administration is now promoting what it calls "transformational diplomacy." Under this new approach to foreign affairs, greater emphasis is placed on the nonmilitary side of international relations. The Bush administration is also revising its national security memorandum that provided the neoconservative blueprint for promoting democracy. The State Department's new emphasis on multilateral negotiations with Iran on its nuclear program shows a new internationalism that the neocons do not support. Furthermore, there is a growing feeling among many Americans that the Defense Department is not the place to invest resources for promoting democracy, economic development, and the rule of law. Perhaps it is time to embrace the lessons of Vietnam and to understand that democracy cannot be imposed by outsiders. Transition to democracy is an evolutionary process that has its own timing, if it comes at all. It will require a multilateral framework, international institutions, and prudent judgment in Washington.[49]

Lyndon Johnson used to say he brought that beautiful lady the Great Society to the ball, but spent all night dancing with that bitch Vietnam. Johnson sacrificed his dreams for a more tolerant and equitable America, one free of the misery of poverty, in the jungles of Vietnam. The neocons seem poised to suffer a similar fate. If there is an Iraq syndrome, the aggressive neoconservative agenda will be lost for a generation of Americans who will have long-lasting memories of getting bogged down in Baghdad. Furthermore, if the Iraq syndrome includes new limits on the use of American power, as it probably will, future policymakers once again will have trouble finding the appropriate balance between ideals and interests. Defending ideals is difficult when the American public wants to retreat from open-ended commitments that have ephemeral, even if noble, goals. One policy analyst believes neoconservatism has become "indelibly associated with concepts like coercive regime change, unilateralism, and American hegemony."[50] If this is true, the lasting legacy of Iraq might be that the United States once again used its power unwisely.

U.S. policymakers went to war in Vietnam and Iraq with the expectation that a distinctively American story would emerge. They believed there were no limits to U.S. power and they could push history along through force. Of course, it is extremely difficult to promote democracy from the barrel of a gun. Americans are also wondering if the United States should take unilateral action in the future against regimes it finds repulsive but that do not represent a direct threat to U.S. national security. Just as in Vietnam, the White House has not made a convincing argument that the nation's security is really at stake in Iraq. In many corners of the country, people suspect the United States cannot solve complicated political problems through military intervention. According to John Mueller, a recent poll in Alabama revealed that 70 percent of those polled would not intervene in Iraq if civil war broke out following a U.S. withdrawal.[51] That the United States is not omnipotent is an important lesson Americans learned in the mangrove swamps and central highlands of Vietnam. It is one the United States is (re)learning in Iraq as well.

ACKNOWLEDGMENTS

In writing this book, I have incurred many debts both personal and intellectual. First on any list must be Deb Sharnak, my excellent research assistant who provided a steady stream of material. I have also drawn a number of ideas from discussions with Fred Logevall, David Elliott, Mai Elliott, Charles Neu, Mark Bradley, David Anderson, and Marilyn Young. Special help in the form of valuable comments on draft chapters came from my colleagues Steve Rock and Norma Torney, and my former mentor George C. Herring. Vietnam's senior foreign-policy scholar, Luu Doan Huynh, shared his ideas with me at key junctures in this project. I am grateful to my colleagues in the History Department at Vassar College who have provided such a supportive intellectual environment. I owe special thanks to Fran Fergusson, Cappy Hill, and Ron Sharp at Vassar, and to Bennett Boskey for his generous support of Vassar and me. I am especially indebted to Peter Osnos, founder of PublicAffairs Books and now its editor-at-large, for his vision and faith in me. Peter is that rare publisher who loves books and ideas. My editor at PublicAffairs, Lindsay Jones, has been supportive of this project from the very beginning. Her good sense and keen mind have made this a better book. Thanks to Scott and Marion Morrison, Brian Trapp, and Bill Kay for pleasant diversions. I want to extend special thanks to my mother, my sister, and the rest of my extended family—the Brigham, Church, and Bradford clans. From the beginning to end of this project, my wife, Monica Church, has shared with me its frustrations and satisfactions. Her own creative and intellectual sensibilities informed many of these pages.

NOTES

Chapter One

1. John Lewis Gaddis, *Surprise, Security, and the American Experience* (Cambridge: Harvard University Press, 2004), p. 13.

2. Walter LaFeber, ed., *John Quincy Adams and American Continental Empire: Letters, Papers, and Speeches* (Chicago: Quadrangle Books, 1965), p. 36.

3. Frederick Jackson Turner, "The Problem of the West," *Atlantic Monthly* 78 (September 1896): 289–297.

4. Dwight D. Eisenhower, *Mandate for Change* (New York: New American Library, 1965), pp. 346–347.

5. Dwight D. Eisenhower, *Public Papers, 1954* (Washington, D.C.: Government Printing Office, 1955), pp. 382–384.

6. Record of telephone conversation, Eisenhower and Dulles, April 5, 1954, Eisenhower Papers, Diary Series, Box 3, Dwight D. Eisenhower Library, Abilene, Kansas.

7. Melvyn Leffler, "9/11 and American Foreign Policy," *Diplomatic History* 29 (June 2005): 395–413.

8. John Foster Dulles, "A Righteous Faith," *Life Magazine* 13 (December 28, 1942): 49–51. See also Seth Jacobs, *America's Miracle Man in Vietnam: Ngo Dinh Diem, Religion, Race, and U.S. Intervention in Southeast Asia* (Durham, N.C.: Duke University Press, 2004), p. 74.

9. John F. Kennedy, "America's Stake in Vietnam," *Vital Speeches* 22 (August 1, 1956): 617–619.

10. George C. Herring, *America's Longest War: The United States and Vietnam, 1950–1975*, 4th ed. (New York: McGraw-Hill, 2002), p. 55.

11. Kennedy to Rusk and McNamara, November 14, 1961, Presidential Office Files, Box 128, John F. Kennedy Library, Boston, Massachusetts.

12. Jonathan Schell, *The Time of Illusion* (New York: Alfred A. Knopf, 1976), pp. 9–10.

13. Theodore C. Sorensen, ed., *Let the Word Go Forth: The Speeches, Statements, and Writings of John F. Kennedy, 1947–1963* (New York: Laurel, 1988), pp. 11–15.

14. Dean Rusk, *As I Saw It: A Secretary of State's Memoirs* (New York: I. B. Tauris, 1991), p. 413.

15. Kennedy to Rusk and McNamara, November 14, 1961, Presidential Office Files, Box 128, John F. Kennedy Library, Boston, Massachusetts.

16. *The Pentagon Papers*, Senator Gravel ed. (Boston: Beacon Press, 1972), vol. 2, p. 111.

17. Fred Logevall, *Choosing War: The Lost Chance for Peace and the Escalation of War in Vietnam* (Berkeley: University of California Press, 1999), p. 31.

18. Thomas Paterson, "Bearing the Burden: A Critical Look at JFK's Foreign Policy," *Virginia Quarterly Review* 54 (Spring 1978): 197.

19. Robert E. Osgood, *Limited War: The Challenge to American Security* (Chicago: University of Chicago Press, 1957); Thomas Schelling, *Arms and Influence* (New Haven: Yale University Press, 1966); and Herman Kahn, *On Escalation* (Baltimore: Penguin Books, 1965).

20. Thomas Schelling, *The Strategy of Conflict* (Cambridge: Harvard University Press, 1960). See also Robert S. McNamara, James G. Blight, and Robert K. Brigham, *Argument Without End: In Search of Answers to the Vietnam Tragedy* (New York: PublicAffairs, 1999), p. 159.

21. McNamara et al., *Argument Without End*, pp. 276–277.

22. Robert S. McNamara, *In Retrospect: The Tragedy and Lessons of Vietnam* (New York: Times Books, 1995), p. 277.

23. McNamara et al., *Argument Without End*, p. 412.

24. Bruce Palmer Jr., *The Twenty-five-Year War: America's Military Role in Vietnam* (Lexington: University of Kentucky Press, 1984), p. 177.

25. See Odd Arne Westad et al., eds., "77 Conversations Between Chinese and Vietnamese Leaders on the Wars in Indochina, 1964–1977," Working Paper no. 22 of the Cold War International History Project (May 1998), Woodrow Wilson Center, Washington, D.C.

26. Alan Whiting, *The Chinese Calculus of Deterrence* (Ann Arbor: University of Michigan Press, 1975), p. 176.

27. Guo Ming et al., *Zhongyue quanxi yanbian sishinian* [Forty-year evolution of Sino-Vietnamese relations] (Nanking: Guangiz People's Press, 1992), p. 69.

28. Chen Jian, "China's Involvement in the Vietnam War, 1964–1969," *China Quarterly* 142 (June 1995): pp. 373–375.

29. Philip Catton, *Diem's Final Failure: Prelude to America's War in Vietnam* (Lawrence: University Press of Kansas, 2002).

30. Robert Topmiller, *The Lotus Unleashed: The Buddhist Movement in South Vietnam, 1964–1966* (Lexington: University of Kentucky Press, 2002).

31. Contacts with Vietnamese Generals, October 23, 1963, Lyndon B. Johnson Papers, Box 2, Lyndon B. Johnson Library, Austin, Texas.

32. Roger Hilsman, *To Move a Nation* (New York: Doubleday, 1967), p. 486.

33. Galbraith to Kennedy, April 4, 1962, Kennedy Papers, National Security File, Box 196, John F. Kennedy Library, Boston, Massachusetts.

34. *Resolution of Ninth Plenum*, Vietnam Documents and Research Notes, Document no. 19, U.S. Mission, Saigon. See also William Duiker, *The Communist Road to Power*, 2d ed. (Boulder, Colo.: Westview Press, 1996), pp. 239–240.

35. Merle L. Pribbenow, *Victory in Vietnam: The Official History of the People's Army of Vietnam, 1954–1975* (Lawrence: University Press of Kansas, 2002), p. 124.

36. As quoted in Herring, *America's Longest War*, p. 113.

37. Memorandum of conversation at the White House, April 4, 1963, *Foreign Relations of the United States, Vietnam, 1961–1963*, vol. 3 (Washington, D.C.: Government Printing Office, 1988), pp. 198–200.

38. McNamara, *In Retrospect*, p. 96.

39. Taylor to Kennedy, November 3, 1961, in *Foreign Relations of the United States, Vietnam, 1961–1963*, vol. 1, pp. 492–493.

40. Chester Cooper, *The Lost Crusade* (New York: Dodd and Mead, 1972), p. 193.

41. McGeorge Bundy memorandum for the record, September 14, 1964, Johnson Papers, National Security File, Country File: Vietnam, Box 6, Lyndon B. Johnson Library, Austin, Texas. See also McNamara to Johnson, April 21, 1965, Johnson Papers, National Security File, Country File: Vietnam, Box 13, Lyndon Johnson Library, Austin, Texas.

42. Herring, *America's Longest War*, p. 138.

43. As quoted in Larry Berman, *Planning a Tragedy: The Americanization of the War in Vietnam* (New York: W. W. Norton, 1982), p. 92.

44. The White House, Press Release, "U.S. Secretary of State Colin Powell Addresses the U.N. Security Council," February 5, 2003.

45. Ibid.

46. Ibid.

47. The White House, Press Release, "President Bush Outlines Iraqi Threat: Remarks by the President on Iraq," Cincinnati Museum Center–Cincinnati Union Terminal, Cincinnati, Ohio, October 7, 2002.

48. The White House, http://www.whitehouse.gov.

49. Ibid.

50. Ibid.

51. Elliot A. Cohen, *Supreme Command: Soldiers, Statesmen, and Leadership in Wartime* (New York: Free Press, 2002).

52. Richard Pipes, "Team B: The Reality Behind the Myth," *Commentary* (October 1986): 25–40; and Murray Friedman, *The Neoconservative Revolution* (Cambridge: Cambridge University Press, 2005).

53. William Kristol and Robert Kagan, *Present Dangers* (San Francisco: Encounter Books, 2000), p. 20.

54. Bill Keller, "The Sunshine Warrior," *New York Times Magazine*, September 22, 2002, p. 50.

55. Ibid., pp. 51–52.

56. Robert W. Tucker and David C. Hendrickson, *Empire of Liberty: The Statecraft of Thomas Jefferson* (New York: Oxford University Press, 1990).

57. Lloyd Gardner, *Safe for Democracy* (New York: Oxford University Press, 1984).

58. N. Gordon Levin Jr., *Woodrow Wilson and World Politics* (New York: Oxford University Press, 1968).

59. Background Information Relating to Southeast Asia and Vietnam, Committee Print, 90th Cong., 1st sess. (Washington, D.C.: Government Printing Office, 1967), pp. 148–153.

60. As quoted in Lloyd Gardner, *Pay Any Price: Lyndon Johnson and the Wars for Vietnam* (Chicago: Ivan R. Dee, 1995), p. 193.

61. Valenti Notes, Johns Hopkins [University] Speech, Johnson Papers, Statements File, Box 143, Lyndon B. Johnson Library, Austin, Texas.

62. Ibid.

63. As quoted in Stanley Karnow, *Vietnam: A History* (New York: Penguin, 1983), p. 419.

64. As quoted in Doris Kearns, *Lyndon Johnson and the American Dream* (New York: Harper and Row, 1976), p. 279.

65. Samuel Huntington, *The Clash of Civilizations and the Remaking of World Order* (New York: Simon and Schuster, 1996).

66. Gaddis, *Surprise, Security, and the American Experience*, pp. 103–104.

67. As quoted in Gardner, *Pay Any Price*, p. 197.

68. Edwin Moise, *Tonkin Gulf and the Escalation of the Vietnam War* (Chapel Hill: University of North Carolina Press, 1996).

69. Eugene Windchy, *Tonkin Gulf* (New York: Doubleday, 1971), p. 24.

70. As quoted in Herring, *America's Longest War*, p. 142.

71. One influential study challenges these claims; see Moise, *Tonkin Gulf*, pp. 142–155.

72. Summary Notes of the 538th Meeting of the National Security Council, August 4, 1964, Johnson Papers, National Security File, NSC Meeting File, Box 1, Lyndon B. Johnson Library, Austin, Texas.

73. Chronology of Events, Tuesday, August 4, and Wednesday, August 5, 1964, Tonkin Gulf Strike, Johnson Papers, National Security File, Country File: Vietnam, Box 18, Lyndon B. Johnson Library, Austin, Texas.

74. Herring, *America's Longest War*, pp. 143–144.

75. Ibid.

76. Chronology of Events, Tuesday, August 4, and Wednesday, August 5, 1964, Tonkin Gulf Strike, Johnson Papers, National Security File, Country File: Vietnam, Box 18, Lyndon B. Johnson Library.

77. William Conrad Gibbons, *The U.S. Government and the Vietnam War: Executive and Legislative Roles and Relationships*, part 2 (Princeton: Princeton University Press, 1986), pp. 297–299.

78. As quoted in Gardner, *Pay Any Price*, p. 134.

79. As quoted in Gibbons, *The U.S. Government and the Vietnam War*, p. 297.

80. McNamara et al., *Argument Without End*, pp. 23–24.

81. McNamara, *In Retrospect*, p. 163.

82. As quoted in Herring, *America's Longest War*, p. 144.

83. Ibid., p. 145.

84. As quoted in Anthony Austin, *The President's War* (Philadelphia: Lippincott, 1971), p. 98.

85. As quoted in Logevall, *Choosing War*, p. 203.

86. John Blum, *Years of Discord: American Politics and Society, 1961–1974* (New York: W. W. Norton, 1991), p. 232.

87. As quoted in Logevall, *Choosing War*, p. 205.

88. Herring, *America's Longest War*, p. 145.

89. White House Press Release, September 30, 2002.

90. White House Press Release, October 1, 2002.

91. Joint Resolution to Authorize the Use of United States Armed Forces in Iraq, White House Press Release, October 2, 2002.

92. Ibid.

93. "War Resolution," White House Press Release, October 16, 2002.

94. Ibid.

95. "Senate Approves Iraq War Resolution," CNN.com, October 11, 2002.

96. "State of the Union Address," White House Press Release, January 29, 2003.

97. Center for Cooperative Research, Press Release, February 20, 2003.

98. "Old Europe Hits Back at Rumsfeld," CNN.com, January 24, 2003.

99. Walter LaFeber, *The American Age: United States Foreign Policy at Home and Abroad Since 1750* (New York: W. W. Norton, 1989), p. 59.

100. "Senate's Roll-Call Vote on King Holiday," *New York Times*, October 20, 1983, p. B9.

Chapter Two

1. "Is Iraq Becoming Another Vietnam?" *USA Today*, April 14, 2004, p. 1A.

2. U.S. Department of Defense, OASD (Comptroller), Directorate of Information Operations, March 19, 1974.

3. New Zealand Embassy, Washington, Records of the New Zealand Ministry of External Relations and Trade, Wellington, New Zealand.

4. Jeffrey Clarke, *Advice and Support: The U.S. Army in Vietnam—The Final Years, 1965–1973* (Washington, D.C.: Center for Military History, 1988), p. 461.

5. Pribbenow, *Victory in Vietnam*, pp. 80–84, 116, 156–157, 182, 191–192, 211, 339, 344–346, 356, 410, 464 fn 14. See also Greg Lockhart, *Nation in Arms: The Origins of the People's Army of Vietnam* (Sydney: Allen and Unwin, 1989), p. 272.

6. Chen Jian, "China's Involvement in the Vietnam War, 1964–1969," *China Quarterly* 142 (June 1995): pp. 373–375.

7. General Vo Nguyen Giap, *Tu nhan dan ma ra* [From the People] (Hanoi: Nha Xuat Ban Su That, 1964).

8. Thom Shanker, "Wolfowitz Testifies Pentagon Misjudged Strength of Iraqi Insurgency," *New York Times*, June 23, 2004, p. A1.

9. Jeffrey Record and W. Andrew Terrill, *Iraq and Vietnam: Differences, Similarities, and Insights* (Carlisle, Penn.: Strategic Studies Institute, 2004), pp. 14–16.

10. Ibid., p. 10; Mark Clodfelter, *The Limits of Air Power: The American Bombing of North Vietnam* (New York: Free Press, 1989), pp. 134, 166, 167, 194; and McNamara et al., *Argument Without End*, p. 379.

11. Record and Terrill, *Iraq and Vietnam*, p. 10. See also Clodfelter, *The Limits of Air Power*, p. 8.

12. McNamara et al., *Argument Without End*, p. 342.

13. Interview with Colin Powell on Frontline, http://www.pbs.org/wgbh/pages/frontline/gulf/oral/powell/1.html.

14. Max Boot, "The New American Way of War," *Foreign Affairs* 82 (July/August 2003): 41–58.

15. Charles Hirschman, Samuel Preston, and Vu Manh Loi, "Vietnamese Casualties During the American War: A New Estimate," *Population and Development Review* 21 (December 1995): 791.

16. Ministry of Labor, War Invalids, and Social Affairs Press Release, Hanoi, Vietnam, April 1995.

17. Department of Defense and Veterans Administration. See also Clarke, *Advice and Support*, p. 275.

18. Ibid.

19. John Clay Thompson, *Operation Rolling Thunder* (Chapel Hill: University of North Carolina Press, 1980); and James William Gibson, *The Perfect War: The War We Couldn't Lose and How We Did* (New York: Vintage, 1986).

20. The British medical journal *Lancet* listed 100,000 Iraqi civilian deaths since March 2003 as reported by the British Broadcasting Corporation (BBC). Information available at http://news.bbc.co.uk/2/hi/middle_east/3962969.stm.

21. Clarke, *Advice and Support*, p. 275.

22. Andrew Krepinevich Jr. "How to Win in Iraq," *Foreign Affairs* 84 (September/October 2005): 91–93.

23. Samuel P. Huntingon, "The Bases of Accommodation," *Foreign Affairs* 46 (July 1968): 652.

24. McGeorge Bundy to President Johnson, January 27, 1965, Memos to the President, Volume 8, January 1–February 28, 1965, Aides Files, McGeorge Bundy, Box 2, Lyndon B. Johnson Library, Austin, Texas.

25. Logevall, *Choosing War*, p. 90.

26. George C. Herring, *LBJ and Vietnam: A Different Kind of War* (Austin: University of Texas Press, 1995), p. 23.

27. McNamara et al., *Argument Without End*, pp. 176–177, 190–191, 193, 354.

28. William Westmoreland, *A Soldier Reports* (Garden City, N.J.: Doubleday, 1976), pp. 168, 170–172, 194.

29. Clifford-Taylor Report, August 5, 1967, Johnson Papers, National Security File, Country File: Vietnam, Box 91, Lyndon B. Johnson Library, Austin, Texas.

30. Herring, *America's Longest War*, p. 183.

31. John Prados, *The Blood Road: The Ho Chi Minh Trail and the Vietnam War* (New York: Wiley and Sons, 1999).

32. Critical Oral Conference on the Vietnam War, June 1997, Hanoi, Vietnam, transcript, Watson Institute, Brown University.

33. Ibid.

34. Herring, *America's Longest War*, p. 184.

35. Malcome Browne, *The New Face of War* (Indianapolis, Ind.: Bobbs-Merrill, 1968), p. ix.

36. William Colby, *Lost Victory: A Firsthand Account of America's Sixteen-Year Involvement in Vietnam* (Chicago: Contemporary Books, 1989), pp. 269–270, 319–320.

37. Melvin Laird, "Iraq: Learning the Lessons of Vietnam," *Foreign Affairs* 84 (November/December 2005): 37.

38. Ibid., p. 26.

39. Matt Steinglass, "Vietnam and Victory," *Boston Globe*, December 18, 2005, pp. 3–4.

40. Ibid.

41. http://www.washingtonpost.com, Sunday, August 8, 1999.

42. Huntington, "The Bases of Accommodation," p. 653.

43. David Elliott, *The Vietnamese War: Revolution and Social Change in the Mekong Delta, 1930–1975*, Vol. 2 (Armonk, N.Y.: M. E. Sharpe, 2003), p. 1169.

44. Lewis Sorley, *A Better War: The Unexamined Victories and Final Tragedy of America's Last Years in Vietnam* (New York: Harcourt Brace, 1999).

45. Henry Kissinger, *Ending the Vietnam War* (New York: Simon and Schuster, 2003), pp. 115, 297–299.

46. Steinglass, "Vietnam and Victory," pp. 3–4.

47. Laird, "Iraq: Learning the Lessons," p. 37.

48. Krepenvich, "How to Win in Iraq," p. 87.

49. Le Duan, "Political Report to the Central Committee of the Lao Dong," in *The Third National Congress of the Vietnam Workers' Party: Documents*, vol. 1 (Hanoi: Foreign Languages Publishing House, 1961), p. 63.

50. Douglas Pike, *Viet Cong: The Organization and Techniques of the National Liberation Front of South Vietnam* (Cambridge: Massachusetts Institute of Technology Press, 1966), pp. 92–93.

51. Ibid., p. 97.

52. Ibid., p. 115.

53. Jeffrey Race, *War Comes to Long An: Revolutionary Conflict in a Vietnamese Province* (Berkeley: University of California Press, 1972), p. 150.

54. For good descriptions of the battle of Ap Bac, see Charles Neu, *America's Lost War* (Wheeling, Ill.: Harlan Davison, 2005), pp. 58–62; Herring, *America's Longest War*, p. 106; Karnow, *Vietnam*, pp. 259–262; Gabriel Kolko, *Anatomy of a War* (New York: Pantheon, 1985), pp. 146–147;

Marilyn Young, *The Vietnam Wars* (New York: Harper Collins, 1991), pp. 89–90; and Neil Sheehan, *A Bright Shining Lie: John Paul Vann and America in Vietnam* (New York: Random House, 1988), pp. 198–199.

55. Hilsman, *To Move a Nation*, pp. 442–456.

56. Ibid., p. 432.

57. See Robert K. Brigham, "Why the South Won the American War in Vietnam," in Marc Gilbert, ed., *Why the North Won the Vietnam War* (New York: Palgrave, 2002), p. 103. See also Duiker, *The Communist Road to Power*, pp. 215–239.

58. Philippe Devillers, "The Struggle for Unification in Vietnam," *China Quarterly* 9 (January–March 1962): 2–23.

59. "A Threat to Peace: North Vietnam's Effort to Conquer South Vietnam," United States State Department, December 1961, Document No. 00358, Douglas Pike Collection, NLF Documents, Indochina Archive, University of California at Berkeley.

60. McNamara et al., *Argument Without End*, p. 321.

61. *U.S.-Vietnam Relations, 1945–1967*, prepared by the Department of Defense and printed by the House Committee on Armed Services, Washington, D.C., 1971, 12 vols.; citation is to vol. 2, section IV.A.5., p. 2.

62. "The Vietnam Workers' Party's 1963 Decision to Escalate the War in the South," *Viet-Nam Documents and Research Notes*, U.S. Mission, Saigon, Document no. 96, July 1971.

63. Nguyen van Hieu, *Ban be ta khap nam chau* [Our friends around the world] (Hanoi: Nha Xuat Ban Van Hoc, 1963).

64. The NLF's Ten-Point Program can be found in translation at http://vietn.vassar.edu/docnlf.html.

65. For a critical description of this belief, see Steven Metz, "Insurgency and Counterinsurgency in Iraq," *Washington Quarterly* 27 (Winter 2003–2004): 26–29.

66. As quoted in Lawrence Kaplan, "Forgetting the Lessons of Vietnam," *New Republic Online*, December 19, 2005.

67. "A Conversation with Colin Powell," *The Atlantic Online* at http://www.theatlantic.com/doc/200408u/powell, August 2, 2004.

68. Lawrence Baskir and William Strauss, *Chance and Circumstance: The Draft, the War, and the Vietnam Generation* (New York: Alfred A. Knopf, 1978), p. 5.

69. Christian Appy, *Working-Class War: American Combat Soldiers and Vietnam* (Chapel Hill: University of North Carolina Press, 1993), p. 18.

70. *U.S. Casualties in Southeast Asia* (Washington, D.C.: Government Printing Office, 1985).

71. John Martin Willis, "Who Died in Vietnam: An Analysis of the Social Background of Vietnam War Casualties," Ph.D. diss., Purdue University, 1975. Ann Arbor, Mich.: University Microfilms.

72. Reports and Statistics Service, Office of Controller, Veterans Administration, April 11, 1972, in Appy, *Working-Class War*, p. 26.

73. *Data on Vietnam-Era Veterans* (Washington, D.C.: Veterans Administration, 1977), p. 12.

74. Fred Worth and Don McCombs, *World War II* (New York: Gramercy, 1994), p. 146.

75. Laird, "Iraq: Learning the Lessons," p. 40.

76. *Data on Vietnam-Era Veterans*, p. 34.

77. David Halbfinger and Steven Holmes, "A Nation at War: The Troops," *New York Times*, March 30, 2003, p. A1.

78. Government Accounting Office Reports, Report no. GAO–05–952, September 22, 2005.

79. Heritage Foundation Reports, "Who Bears the Burden? Demographic Characteristics of U.S. Military Recruits Before and After 9/11," November 7, 2005.

80. Government Accounting Office Reports, no. GAO–05–952.

81. *The Gallup Opinion Index: Political, Social, and Economic Trends*. A monthly publication, giving in considerable detail the results of Gallup polls on various issues.

82. Ibid. See also Richard A. Brody et al., *Public Opinion and the War in Vietnam* (ICPR Study 7295) (Ann Arbor, Mich.: Inter-University Consortium for Political Research, 1972), reprinted 1975.

83. *The Gallup Opinion Index*.

84. Peter J. Boyer, "The Believer: Paul Wolfowitz Defends His War," *The New Yorker*, November 1, 2004.

85. CNN-Gallup Poll, January 6–8, 2006, compiled by the Pew Charitable Trust.

86. Ibid.

Chapter Three

1. Transcript of presidential debates, Commission on Presidential Debates, online at http://www.debates.org/pages/trans2000a.html.

2. "Elections in Iraq," *Washington Post*, December 15, 2005, p. A32.

3. International Information Programs, United States Information Agency, January 17, 2005.

4. Lawrence Freedman, "Writings of Wrongs," *Foreign Affairs* 85 (January/February 2006): 132.

5. Paul Pillar, "Intelligence, Policy, and the War in Iraq," *Foreign Affairs* 85 (March/April 2006): 16.

6. "Turf Wars and the Future of Iraq," Frontline online at http://www.pbs.org/wgbh/pages/frontline/shows/truth/fighting/turfwars.html.

7. Ibid.

8. Ibid.

9. Ibid.

10. Ibid.

11. Rand Corporation, "America's Role in Nation-Building: From Germany to Iraq," Santa Monica, Calif., March 2003.

12. Dominique Vidal, "A Guide to Nation-Building," *Le Monde diplomatique* (December 2003): 1.

13. Rand, "America's Role in Nation-Building, p. xxvii.

14. Ibid.

15. See Douglas Porch, "Review, James Dobbins' 'America's Role in Nation-building: From Germany to Iraq,'" *Strategic Insights* 3 (February 2004): 14.

16. Benedict Anderson, *Imagined Communities: Reflections on the Origin and Spread of Nationalism* (London: Verso, 1991).

17. Eric Hobsbawm, *Nations and Nationalism Since 1780: Programme, Myth, and Reality* (Cambridge: Cambridge University Press, 1990); and Eric Hobsbawm and Terence Ranger, *The Invention of Tradition* (Cambridge: Cambridge University Press, 1983).

18. Ernest Renan, "What Is a Nation?" trans. and anno. Martin Thom, in Geoff Eley and Renald Grigor Suny, eds., *Becoming National: A Reader* (New York: Oxford University Press, 1996), p. 52.

19. Michael Howard, *The Lessons of History* (New Haven: Yale University Press, 1991), p. 2.

20. Barbara Ehrenreich, *Blood Rites: Origins and History of the Passions of War* (New York: Henry Holt, 1997), p. 200.

21. Niall Ferguson, "Op-ed," *New York Times*, April 18, 2004, p. A43.

22. Critical Oral Conference on the Vietnam War, transcript, Watson Institute, Brown University.

23. *May van de tong ket chien tranh va viet lich su quan su* [Selected issues related to the conclusions and the writing of the military history of the war] (Hanoi: Nha Xuat Ban Su That, 1987); Pham van Dong, "Phat huy chu nghia anh hung cach mang, day manh su nghiep chong My, cuu nuoc den thang loi hoan toan [Promote revolutionary heroism, strengthen the anti-U.S. resistance war for national salvation of the fatherland to lead to complete victory] *Hoc Tap* 13 (January 1967): 17–20; and Robert K. Brigham, "Revolutionary Heroism and Politics in Postwar Vietnam," in Charles Neu, ed., *After Vietnam: Legacies of a Lost War* (Baltimore: Johns Hopkins University Press, 2000), pp. 85–104.

24. Frances FitzGerald, *Fire in the Lake: The Vietnamese and the Americans in Vietnam* (New York: Vintage, 1972), p. 512.

25. William Duiker, *Vietnam: Revolution in Transition*, 2d ed. (Boulder, Colo.: Westview Press, 1995), p. 123.

26. Ronald Spector, *Advice and Support: The Early Years of the U.S. Army in Vietnam, 1941–1960* (New York: Free Press, 1985), p. 237.

27. Record and Terrill, *Iraq and Vietnam*, p. 45.

28. Anthony Cordesman, *The Iraq War: Strategy, Tactics, and Military Lessons* (Washington, D.C.: Center for Strategic and International Studies, 2002), p. 554. See also Jeffrey Record, *Dark Victory: America's Second War with Iraq* (Annapolis: Naval Institute Press, 2003), pp. 141–142.

29. Stephen Biddle, "Seeing Baghdad, Thinking Saigon," *Foreign Affairs* 85 (March/April 2006): 8.

30. Ibid., p. 9.

31. Clarke, *Advice and Support*, pp. 161–163.

32. General Duong van Khuyen, *RVNAF* (Washington, D.C.: Center for Military History, 1988), pp. 181–182.

33. Laird, "Iraq: Learning the Lessons," p. 29.

34. "President Richard Nixon's Speech to the Nation on Vietnam, November 3, 1969," *Public Papers of President Richard Nixon, 1969* (Washington, D.C.: Government Printing Office, 1970), p. 431.

35. Political Transcript Wire, Lanham, December 2, 2005, wire feed.

36. White House Press Release, President Bush Speech before Veterans of Foreign Wars, January 10, 2006.

37. Ibid.

38. "General Says Training of Iraqi Troops Suffered from Poor Planning and Staffing," *New York Times*, February 11, 2006, p. A6.

39. Ibid.

40. Ibid.

41. Ibid.

42. *The Pentagon Papers: The Secret History of the Vietnam War, as published by the New York Times* (New York: Bantam Books, 1971), p. 420.

43. Deployment of Forces, Saigon to Washington, June 5, 1965, National Security File, NSC History, Box 4, Lyndon B. Johnson Library, Austin, Texas.

44. *The Pentagon Papers*, pp. 419–420.

45. General William Westmoreland, *Report on Operations in South Vietnam, January 1964–June 1968*, Center for Military History (Washington, D.C.: Government Printing Office, 1969), p. 109.

46. Herring, *America's Longest War*, pp. 166–167.

47. Clarke, *Advice and Support*, p. 463.

48. Ibid., p. 503.

49. Ibid.

50. General Duong van Khuyen, *RVNAF*.

51. Central Intelligence Agency, *World Fact Book on Iraq*, 2005.

52. Ibid.

53. Ibid.

54. Bob Herbert, "The Destroyers," *New York Times*, February 13, 2006, p. A23.

55. Ibid.

56. Biddle, "Seeing Baghdad, Thinking Saigon," p. 8.

57. Ibid.

58. Eric Schmitt, "Iraq-Bound Marine Leaders Cram on Civics and Economics," *New York Times*, February 13, 2006, p. A8.

59. "Elections in Iraq," *Washington Post*, December 15, 2005, p. A32.

60. Walt Rostow, *The Process of Economic Growth* (New York: W. W. Norton, 1952).

61. Ibid.

62. Laird, "Iraq: Learning the Lessons of Vietnam," p. 35.

63. Tran van Don, *Our Endless War Inside Vietnam* (San Rafael, Calif.: Presidio Press, 1978), p. 241.

64. Malcom Browne, "Deep Recession Grips Saigon," *New York Times*, June 4, 1972, p. A1.

65. Sabrina Tavernise, "As Iraqi Shiites Police Sunnis, Rough Justice Feeds Bitterness," *New York Times*, February 6, 2006, p. A1.

66. Ibid.

67. John Mueller, "The Iraq Syndrome," *Foreign Affairs* 84 (November/December 2005): 50.

68. Fareed Zakaria, *The Future of Freedom: Illiberal Democracy at Home and Abroad* (New York: W. W. Norton, 2003).

69. Ibid.

Chapter Four

1. Gardner, *Pay Any Price*, p. 297.

2. Mueller, "The Iraq Syndrome," p. 44.

3. Ibid.

4. Hazel Erskine, "The Polls: Is War a Mistake?" *Public Opinion Quarterly* 34 (Spring 1970): 134–150.

5. Pew Research Center for the People and the Press, "The Public Struggles with Possible War in Iraq," January 30, 2003.

6. Susan Page, "Poll: American Attitudes on Iraq Similar to Vietnam Era," *USA Today*, November 15, 2005, p. 1.

7. *Gallup Poll: Public Opinion 1935–1971*, 3 vols. (New York: Random House, 1972). 1972–1977 and later volumes: (Wilmington, Del.: Scholarly Resources).

8. Mueller, "The Iraq Syndrome," p. 45.

9. Ibid.

10. As quoted in Mueller, "The Iraq Syndrome," p. 45.

11. Ibid.

12. "The War in Vietnam," Draft no. 1, Johnson Papers, Statement File, Box 143, Lyndon B. Johnson Library, Austin, Texas.

13. Ibid.

14. "Second Draft, March 20, 1968," Johnson Papers, NSC Histories, Box 128, Lyndon B. Johnson Library, Austin, Texas.

15. Ibid.

16. As quoted in Richard Stebbins, *The United States in World Affairs 1967* (New York: Council on Foreign Relations; Simon and Schuster, 1968), p. 68.

17. Herring, *America's Longest War*, pp. 220–221.

18. Walt Rostow to Ellsworth Bunker, September 27, 1967, Johnson Papers, DSDUF, Box 4, Lyndon B. Johnson Library, Austin, Texas.

19. Depuy to Westmoreland, October 19, 1967, William Depuy Papers, Folder WXYZ–67, U.S. Army Military History Institute, Carlisle Barracks, Penn.

20. *Tet mau than 68* [Tet 1968] (Hanoi: Ban Tuyen Huan Trung Uong, 1988).

21. Louis Harris, *The Anguish of Change* (New York: W. W. Norton, 1973), pp. 63–64. See also Burns Roper, "What Public Opinion Polls Said," in Peter Braestrup, ed., *Big Story: How the American Press and Television Reported and Interpreted the Crisis of Tet in 1968 in Vietnam and Washington* (Boulder, Colo.: Westview Press, 1977), vol. 2, pp. 674–704.

22. As quoted in Don Oberdorfer, *Tet!* (Garden City, N.Y.: Doubleday, 1971), p. 158.

23. Robert Elegant, "How to Lose a War," *Encounter* 57 (August 1981): 73–90.

24. As reported in Jay Rosen, "The News from Iraq Is Not Too Negative, but It Is Too Narrow," *Pressthink*, May 26, 2004, p. 2.

25. Michael Massing, "Now They Tell Us," *New York Review of Books* 51 (February 26, 2004): 34–35.

26. Karnow, *Vietnam*, p. 262.

27. William Prochnau, *Once upon a Distant War: David Halberstam, Neil Sheehan, Peter Arnett—Young War Correspondents and Their Early Vietnam Battles* (New York: Times Books, 1995), p. 232.

28. Ibid., p. 235.

29. Neil Sheehan, "Costly Vietnam Battle Angers U.S. Advisers," *Washington Post*, January 4, 1963, p. 1.

30. Neil Sheehan, "Vietnamese Ignored U.S. Battle Order," *Washington Post*, January 7, 1963, p. 1. For a reprint of the article, see *Reporting Vietnam* (New York: Library of America, 1998), pp. 68–70.

31. David Halberstam, "Vietcong Downs Five U.S. Copters, Hits Nine Others," *New York Times*, January 3, 1963, p. 1.

32. David Halberstam, "Vietnamese Reds Win Major Clash," *New York Times*, January 4, 1963, p. 2.

33. David Halberstam, "Vietnam Defeat Shocks U.S. Aides," *New York Times*, January 6, 1963, p. 2.

34. See *Reporting Vietnam*, pp. 68–70.

35. Prochnau, *Once upon a Distant War*, p. 239.

36. Ibid., p. 240.

37. *Foreign Relations of the United States, Vietnam, 1961–1963: January-August 1963* (Washington, D.C.: Government Printing Office, 1991), vol. 3, p. 3.

38. David Halberstam, *The Making of a Quagmire* (New York: Random House, 1965), p. 158.

39. Interestingly, many authors have suggested Felt's comments were directed at others, not Malcome Browne. Stanley Karnow suggests the remark was meant for Peter Arnett of the Associated Press; Karnow, *Vietnam*, pp. 260–262. John Clarke Pratt says Felt directed his response at Neil Sheehan of the United Press International; John Clarke Pratt, *Vietnam Voices* (New York: Penguin, 1984), pp. 126–127. Prochnau claims Browne was indeed the intended recipient of Felt's anger.

40. Critical Oral Conference on the Vietnam War, transcript, Watson Institute, Brown University.

41. As quoted in Karnow, *Vietnam*, p. 487.

42. *Gallup Poll: Public Opinion 1935–1971*, vol. 3.

43. *Public Papers of the President, Richard M. Nixon, 1969* (Washington, D.C.: Government Printing Office, 1971), pp. 901–909.

44. Ibid.

45. Charles Babington, "Hawkish Democrat Joins Call for Pullout," *Washington Post*, November 18, 2005, p. A1.

46. As quoted in John Mulligan, "Historians, Soldiers Hesitant to Call Iraq Another Vietnam," *Providence Journal*, April 25, 2004, p. A8.

47. Ibid.

48. Ibid.

49. Bartholomew Sullivan, "The Road from Tet to Fallujah," *Commercial Appeal,* May 30, 2004, p. B3.

50. Susan Page, "Is Iraq Becoming Another Vietnam?" *USA Today,* April 14, 2004, p. 1A.

51. Bob Herbert, *New York Times,* September 27, 2004, p. A27.

52. Robert Kutner, *Washington Post,* November 7, 2004, p. B7.

53. Lawrence Freedman, "Rumsfeld's Legacy: The Iraq Syndrome?" *Washington Post,* January 9, 2005, p. B5.

54. Babington, "Hawkish Democrat Joins Call," p. A1.

55. Ibid.

56. "Cheney Calls War Critics 'Opportunists,'" MSNBC News Service, 9:00 A.M., November 17, 2005.

57. Babington, "Hawkish Democrat Joins Call," p. A1.

58. Jonathan Rauch, "Iraq Is No Vietnam, but Vietnam Holds Lessons for Iraq," *National Journal* 36 (September 11, 2004): 2710–2711.

59. Anthony Zinni, "Making Vietnam's Mistakes All over Again," *New Perspectives Quarterly* 21 (Summer 2004): 24–28.

60. Barbara Slavin, "McCain: Force Levels in Iraq Inadequate," *USA Today,* November 5, 2003, p. A1.

61. Ibid.

62. Gary Jacobson, a political scientist at the University of California at San Diego, has studied this partisan divide. See Michael Fletcher, "Iraq Critics Meet Familiar Reply, White House Reverts to Blistering Attacks of 2004 Campaign," *Washington Post,* November 18, 2005, p. A6.

63. Ibid.

64. Quoted in Thomas Powers, *Vietnam: The War at Home* (New York: Grossman, 1973), p. 118.

65. Melvin Small, *Johnson, Nixon, and the Doves* (New Brunswick, N.J.: Rutgers University Press, 1988), p. 60.

66. Sidney Verba et al., "Public Opinion and the War in Vietnam," *American Political Science Review* 61 (June 1967): 317–333; and Peter Sperlich and William Lunch, "American Public Opinion and the War in Vietnam," *Western Political Quarterly* 32 (March 1979): 21–44.

67. Critical Oral Conference on the Vietnam War, transcript, Watson Institute, Brown University.

68. Charles DeBenedetti, *An American Ordeal: The Antiwar Movement of the Vietnam Era* (Syracuse, N.Y.: Syracuse University Press, 1990), pp. 203–204.

69. Rowland Evans and Robert Novak, "Johnson's Home Front," *Washington Post*, July 30, 1965, p. 1.

70. Notes on Meeting with Congressional Leadership, January 25, 1966, Johnson Papers, Meeting Notes File, Box 1, Lyndon Johnson Library, Austin, Texas. See also Herring, *America's Longest War*, p. 205.

71. Herring, *America's Longest War*, p. 278.

72. Critical Oral Conference on the Vietnam War, transcript, Watson Institute, Brown University.

73. Logevall, *Choosing War*, pp. 272–273.

74. Memorandum from the Secretary of State to the President, January 8, 1964, *Foreign Relations of the United States, Vietnam, 1964–1968*, vol. 1 (Washington, D.C.: Government Printing Office, 1992), pp. 9–10.

75. Logevall, *Choosing War*, p. 373.

76. Critical Oral Conference on the Vietnam War, transcript, Watson Institute, Brown University.

77. As quoted in Gardner, *Pay Any Price*, p. 315.

78. As quoted in Kearns, *Lyndon Johnson and the American Dream*, pp. 263–265, 272.

79. Herring, *America's Longest War*, p. 136.

80. As quoted in ibid., p. 136.

81. Brian VanDeMark, *Into the Quagmire* (New York: Oxford University Press, 1990), pp. xv, 60.

82. Michael Beschloss, *Taking Charge: The Johnson White House Tapes* (New York: Simon and Schuster, 1998), p. 403.

83. Herring, *America's Longest War*, p. 138.

84. McNamara et al., *Argument Without End*, p. 292.

85. *The Pentagon Papers: United States–Vietnam Relations, 1945–1967, Study Presented by the Department of Defense* (Washington, D.C.: Government Printing Office, 1971), vol. 6, pp. 124–125.

86. McNamara, *In Retrospect*, p. 286.

87. Herring, *America's Longest War*, p. 215.

88. McNamara, *In Retrospect*, p. 307.

89. Richard Helms, Memorandum for the President, September 12, 1967, Country File: Vietnam, National Security Files, Box 259/260, Lyndon B. Johnson Library, Austin, Texas.

90. Laird, "Iraq: Learning the Lessons," p. 27.

91. As reported in Steve Grove, "The Question on the Corner," *Boston Globe*, May 2, 2004, p. 1.

92. Mueller, "The Iraq Syndrome," p. 46.

93. China, Dr. Kissinger's Visit, June 1972 Memcons Folder, National Security Council, Kissinger Office Files, Box 97 and Polo I, Kissinger Briefing Book, July 1971 Trip to China, National Security Council, Box 850, Nixon Presidential Materials Project, National Archives and Records Administration, College Park, Md.

94. As quoted in Jussi Hanhimaki, *The Flawed Architect: Henry Kissinger and American Foreign Policy* (New York: Oxford University Press, 2004), p. 225.

95. Memorandum of Conversation, 20 June 1972, 2:05–6:06 P.M., Great Hall of the People, China, Dr. Kissinger's Visit, June 1972 Memcons folder, National Security Council, Kissinger Office Files, Box 97, Nixon Presidential Materials Project, National Archives and Records Administration, College Park, Md.

96. Ibid.

97. Ibid.

98. "Conversation 760–766, 3 August 1972, 8:28–8:57 A.M., Oval Office," Nixon Presidential Materials Project, National Archives and Records Administration, College Park, Md.

99. Luu van Loi and Nguyen Anh Vu, *Le Duc Tho–Kissinger negotiations in Paris* (Hanoi: Gioi Publishers, 1996), pp. 188–191.

100. Critical Oral Conference on the Vietnam War, transcript, Watson Institute, Brown University.

101. As quoted in Karnow, *Vietnam*, p. 636.

102. Herring, *America's Longest War*, pp. 246–247.

103. Acheson to John Cowles, March 14, 1968, Dean Acheson Papers, Yale University Library, Box 7, New Haven, Conn.

104. Terry Anderson, *The Movement and the Sixties: Protest in America from Greensboro to Wounded Knee* (New York: Oxford University Press, 1995), pp. 178–179.

Chapter Five

1. Francis Fukuyama, "After Neoconservatism," *New York Times Magazine*, February 19, 2006, p. 65.

2. "An Irony of History," *Newsweek*, April 28, 1975, p. 17.

3. Herring, *America's Longest War*, p. 346.

4. Ibid., p. 349.

5. *New Orleans Times Picayune*, April 23, 1975, p. 1.

6. Notes on cabinet meeting, April 16, 1975, Ron Nessen Papers, Box 294; Memorandum of conversation, Kissinger, Ford, and congressional leaders, March 5, 1975, Kissinger/Scowcroft File, Box A1, Gerald Ford Library, Ann Arbor, Mich.

7. *Congressional Record*, 94th Cong., 1st sess., pp. 10101–10108.

8. Quoted in Neu, *America's Lost War*, p. 225.

9. Paul Kennedy, *The Rise and Fall of the Great Powers* (New York: Random House, 1987), pp. 408.

10. Quoted in Thomas Franck and Edward Weisband, *Foreign Policy by Congress* (New York: Oxford University Press, 1979), p. 46.

11. Quoted in the *Washington Post*, January 12, 1977, p. 1.

12. *Public Papers of the President, Jimmy Carter, 1980–1981*, vol. 1 (Washington, D.C.: Government Printing Office, 1981), p. 197.

13. *Department of State Bulletin* 80 (February 1980): Special B.

14. As quoted in Thomas Paterson et al., *American Foreign Policy*, 3d ed. (Lexington, Mass.: D. C. Heath, 1991), p. 641.

15. Quoted in Gaddis Smith, *Morality, Reason, and Power* (New York: Hill and Wang, 1986), p. 232.

16. Mueller, "The Iraq Syndrome," p. 53.

17. LaFeber, *The American Age*, pp. 665–666.

18. Smith, *Morality, Reason, and Power*, pp. 9, 81–84.

19. LaFeber, *The American Age*, p. 666.

20. Neu, *America's Lost War*, p. 227.

21. Edward Coffman, "The Course of Military History in the United States Since World War II," *Journal of Military History* 61 (October 1997): 769–770.

22. George Herring, "Preparing Not to Refight the Last War: The Impact of the Vietnam War on the U.S. Military," in Charles Neu, ed., *After*

Vietnam: Legacies of a Lost War (Baltimore, Md.: Johns Hopkins University Press, 2000), p. 65.

23. Lewis Sorley, *Thunderbolt: General Creighton Abrams and the Army of His Times* (New York: Simon and Schuster, 1992), pp. 360–365.

24. Herring, "Preparing Not to Refight the Last War," p. 65.

25. Quoted in Neu, *America's Lost War*, p. 229.

26. Cohen, *Supreme Command.*

27. Colin Powell, "U.S. Forces: Challenges Ahead," *Foreign Affairs* 71 (Winter 1992/1993): 37.

28. News Conference with President Bush, Federal News Service, August 7, 1992.

29. As quoted in Samantha Power, *A Problem from Hell: America and the Age of Genocide* (New York: Perennial, 2002), p. 284.

30. Ibid.

31. B. Drummond Ayres, "In American Voices, a Sense of Concern over Bosnia Role," *New York Times*, May 2, 1993, p. 4.

32. Gaddis, *Surprise, Security, and the American Experience*, pp. 77–78.

33. Francis Fukuyama, *The End of History and the Last Man* (New York: Free Press, 1992).

34. Power, *A Problem from Hell*, pp. 283–285, 294, 315.

35. Henry Kissinger, *Diplomacy* (New York: Simon and Schuster, 1994), p. 803.

36. William Kristol and Lawrence Kaplan, *The War over Iraq* (San Francisco: Encounter Books, 2003), p. 47.

37. As quoted in Fukuyama, "After Neoconservatism," p. 66.

38. Max Boot, "The Case for an American Empire," *Weekly Standard*, October 15, 2001. See also Boot, *The Savage Wars for Peace: Small Wars and the Rise of American Power* (New York: Basic Books, 2002); and Niall Ferguson, *Colossus: The Price of America's Empire* (New York: Penguin, 2004).

39. Richard Clarke, *Against All Enemies: Inside America's War on Terror* (New York: Free Press, 2004).

40. Kristol and Kaplan, *The War over Iraq*, p. 112.

41. Gaddis, *Surprise, Security, and the American Experience*, p. 81.

42. As quoted in Wesley Clark, *Winning Modern Wars: Iraq, Terrorism, and the American Empire* (New York: PublicAffairs, 2003), p. 163.

43. Second Bush Inaugural, White House Press Release.

44. Clark, *Winning Modern Wars,* p. 164.

45. Ibid.

46. Fukuyama, "After Neoconservatism," p. 65.

47. As described in Edward Luttwak, "Iraq: The Logic of Disengagement," *Foreign Affairs* 84 (January/February 2005): 26.

48. Fukuyama, "After Neoconservatism," p. 63.

49. Ibid.

50. Ibid., p. 67.

51. Mueller, "The Iraq Syndrome," p. 53.

INDEX

Abizaid, John, 115
Abrams, Creighton, 47, 49–50, 51, 151
Abu Ghraib prison scandal, 67, 109
Acheson, Dean, 132
Adair, Ross, 24
Adams, John, 29
Adams, John Quincy, 1–2, 30
Afghanistan, 17, 28, 74, 144, 158
Aiken, George, 122
Ali, Husayn ibn, 75–76
al-Qaeda
    Hussein, Saddam and, x, 31
    Iraq and, 13, 14, 26
    Iraq insurgency and, 59
American Friends of Vietnam, 4
"America's Role in National-Building:
    From Germany to Iraq," 73
Anderson, Benedict, 74
Ansar al-Islam, 58
anti-Americanism, 59, 60
Associated Press, 111
Australia, 36
Ayres, Drummond, 155

Baathists, 80, 81, 82
Balkans, xv, 154–55, 156, 161
Baltimore Sun, 48
Beirut, Lebanon, 147, 148
Bell, Daniel, 16
A Better War (Sorley), 49
Biddle, Stephen, 81, 93
bin Laden, Osama, 13, 26, 158
Blair, Tony, 29
*Blood Rites: Origins and History of the
    Passions of War* (Ehrenreich), 75
Boot, Max, 158
Bosnia, 74, 155
Boston Globe, 48
Boyer, Peter J., 66
Bremer, Paul, 72–73
Britain
    Turkey and, 75–76
    War in Iraq and, 29
Browne, Malcom, 47, 111
Buddhists, 9, 97
Bundy, McGeorge, 141–42
Bunker, Ellsworth, 130

Burma, 4

Bush, George H. W., xiv–xv
  First Gulf War (1990–1991) and, 15,
    39, 152
  foreign policy of, 161
  Vietnam Syndrome and, 152–53

Bush, George W.
  approval ratings of, 116
  Bush Doctrine and, 14–17
  idealism and, 161–62
  national security and, ix
  nation building and, xi, 20, 69–70,
    75, 79
  September 11 and, 160
  U. S. power and, xiv, 138
  War in Iraq, support for and, xii,
    25–28, 103–06,
  War on Terror and, 160–61

Byrd, Robert, 27, 113

Cambodia, xv, 4, 46, 52, 118, 119, 127,
    144–45

Can Lao Party, 97–98

Carter, Jimmy, 116
  foreign policy of, 142–46

Carter Doctrine, 143

"The Case for an American Empire"
    (Boot), 158

Castro, Fidel, 60

Central Intelligence Agency (CIA),
    23, 39, 72, 130

Cheney, Dick, 114–15

Chiarelli, Peter, 94

China, xi, 143
  Vietnam War and, xi, 8–9, 37

Chinese Communists, 53

Church, Frank, 119

CIA. See Central Intelligence
    | Agency

Clark, Wesley, 162

Clarke, Jeffrey, 91

Clausewitz, Carl von, 150

"clear and hold" strategy, 47, 48

Clinton, Bill, 116
  foreign policy of, 155–58, 161

Coalition Provisional Authority
    (CPA), 72

Cohen, Elliot, 15

cold war, 3
  foreign policy and, 7
  national security and, 7
  neoconservatives and, 17
  Vietnam War and, x

Committee for Peace with Freedom,
    107

communism
  credibility, theory of and, 9
  democracy and, 2
  domino theory and, 3–4
  in Southeast Asia, x, 2
  Vietnam War and, x, 2, 19

Congress
  power and, 3
  Vietnam War and, xii, 21–22,
    24–25, 30, 116–18
  War in Iraq and, xii, 25–29, 30, 103,
    113–16
  War on Terror and, 159–60

containment, 12, 143

Cooper, John Sherman, 119

credibility, theory of, 5–6, 9, 11, 12, 31,
    120–25

Cronkite, Walter, 108

C. Turner Joy, 22, 23

Daschle, Tom, 27–28
Davis, Nathaniel, 142
"decent interval," xii–xiii, 125, 127,
128, 129, 164
Defense Department, 38, 65, 166
DeLay, Tom, 27
democracy
communism and, 2
expansionism and, 2
in Middle East, xii, xv, 15–16, 17, 31,
104
national security and, xiii, 15, 18,
138
nation building and, 70, 71, 93–94,
99–102
neoconservatives and, 137, 163,
165–66
terrorism and, 20
in Vietnam, 101–2
Democratic Party, Democrats
domino theory and, 4
Vietnam War and, 118
War in Iraq and, 27
Dempsey, Martin, 85
détente, 16, 143, 157
Diem, Ngo Dinh
. See Ngo Dinh Diem
diplomacy, 8, 148
transformational, 165
domino theory, 3–6, 31
communism and, 3–4
Kennedy, John F. and, 4, 5, 9
legitimacy of, 4
"psychological," 5–6, 122–23
Doung van Minh, 130
Duiker, William, 77–78
Dulles, John Foster, 3–4, 5

Eaton, Paul, 85–86
Ehrenreich, Barbara, 75
Eisenhower, Dwight D., 2, 3
foreign policy of, 6–7
Geneva accords (1954) and, 5
New Look policy of, 7
Vietnam War and, 4, 5
Elliott, David, 48
expansionism
democracy and, 2
national security and, 1–2, 30
Vietnam War and, 31

Faysal, Prince, 76
Faysal II, King, 89–90
Felt, Harry, 111
Ferguson, Niall, 75
First Gulf War (1990–1991), 13, 15, 152
Bush, George H. W. and, 15, 39
exit strategy in, xiv
goals of, xiv
Hussein, Saddam and, xiv, 152–54
limited nature of, xiv
Powell, Colin and, xiv
Vietnam Syndrome and, 152–54
FitzGerald, Frances, 77
Ford, Gerald, 140
Ford, Harold, Jr., 113
Foreign Affairs, 47, 70, 84, 93
foreign policy
cold war, 7
containment, 12, 143
credibility, theory of and, 5–6, 9,
11, 12, 31, 120–25
"decent interval" and, 126, 127,
128, 129, 164
détente, 16, 143, 157

foreign policy (*cont.*)
  diplomacy and, 8, 148, 165
  domino theory and, 3–6, 9, 31,
    122–23
  expansionism and, 1–2, 30, 31
  human rights and, 155–56
  Iraq Syndrome and, xiv, xv,
    163–67
  preemption and, 2, 31
  U. S. power and, xv
  Vietnam Syndrome and, xiv, xv,
    140–61
  Vietnam War and, 139–40
  War in Iraq and, ix, xi
  Weinberger Doctrine and,
    146–49
France, Vietnam and, 4–5, 80
Franks, Tommy, 115
Freedman, Lawrence, 114
Fukuyama, Francis, 104, 163
Fulbright, J. William, 24–25, 117
Future of Iraq Project, 71–72, 93

Gaddis, John Lewis, 20, 160
Garner, Jay, 71–72
Geneva accords (1954), 5, 55
George, Lloyd, 75
Gephardt, Richard, 27
Glazer, Nathan, 16
Goldwater-Nichols Reorganization
    Act (1986), 64, 151–52
Gore, Al, 69, 157
Great Society, 117, 131, 132
Gruening, Ernest, 24
Gulf of Tonkin Resolution (1964),
    24–25, 29, 32, 119

Hadid, Umar Husayn, 58
Hagel, Chuck, 116
Hai Ba Trung, 76
Hakim, Abdel 'Aziz al-, 58
Halberstam, David, 110, 111
Hamas, 31
Hamlet Evaluation Survey (HES), 49
Harkins, Paul, 111
Harriman, W. Averell, 132
Hatfield, Mark, 119
Helms, Richard, 123–24
Herbert, Bob, 92–93, 114
Herring, George C., 22, 139, 152
HES. *See* Hamlet Evaluation Survey
Hilsman, Roger, 54
HJ114, 27
Hobsbawm, Eric, 74
Ho Chi Minh, x, 55
  Mekong River Development Pro-
    ject and, 21, 44
  as national symbol, 56–57, 77–78
  nationhood and, 76
  tyranny of, 2
  Vietnamese Communists of, 2,
    4–5, 12
  Vietnamese insurgency and, 59,
    60
Ho Chi Minh Trail, 38, 46, 56, 122
Howard, Michael, 75
Howe, Irving, 16
human rights, 155–56
Humphrey, Hubert, 89
Huntington, Samuel, 20
Hurricane Katrina, 131
Hussein, Saddam, xiii
  al-Qaeda and, x, 31
  Baathists and, 80, 81, 82
  First Gulf War (1990–1991) and,

xiv, 152–54
sanctions against, 71
terrorism and, 15, 28
War in Iraq and, 26
WMDs and, 2, 13, 26, 28

Iraq Syndrome, xiv, xv, 126, 163–67
Iron Curtain, 6
Isaacs, Arnold, 48
isolationism, 164–65
Israel, 26, 152

idealism, xiii
    Bush, George W. and, 161–62
    power and, 3
    U. S. power and, 138
    Vietnam War and, 1, 5, 18–21, 138,
        139
    War in Iraq and, xiv, 1, 138
Ikle, Fred, 16
Indochina, 4, 5
Institute for Defense Analyses, 38
international community
    Ho Chi Minh and, 57
    War in Iraq and, 28
internationalism, 157, 158
Iran, 166
Iran hostage crisis (1979), 144
Iraq
    al-Qaeda and, 13, 14, 26
    insurgency in, ix, xi, 13–14, 52,
        56–62
    international terrorism and, 2, 26
    as modern nation-state, 75–76
    national army in, 79–82, 82–84,
        85–87, 89–90
    nation building in, xi, xv, 20,
        69–76, 79–82, 84–87, 89–90,
        92–102, 115
    regime change in, 12, 17, 138
    socioeconomic viability and, 92–95
    terrorism and, xii, 28
Iraqi Islamic Party, 99

Jaafari, Ibrahim al-, 130–131
Jackson, Henry "Scoop", 16
Jacobson, Gary, 116
Japan, 4, 74, 159
JASON study, 38–39, 123
Javits, Jacob, 118
Jefferson, Thomas, 1, 18
Johnson, Lyndon B.
    American ideals, exporting and,
        18–21
    credibility, theory of and, 120–24
    Great Society of, 117, 131, 132
    liberal press and, 111–12
    U. S. power and, xii–xiv, 138
    Vietnam economic development
        and, 95–96
    Vietnam War, funding and,
        131–33
    Vietnam War, opposition to and,
        116–18
    Vietnam War, public support for
        and, xii, 103–8, 111–12
    Vietnam War and, 11–12, 44

Kagan, Robert, 17, 158
Kahn, Herman, 7
Kaplan, Lawrence, 158, 160
Karadzic, Radovan, 154
Katzenbach, Nicholas, 123
Kennan, George F., 105, 144

Kennedy, Edward, 27, 113
Kennedy, John F.
    assassination of, 11
    credibility, theory of and, 5–6, 9
    domino theory and, 4, 5, 9, 31
    foreign policy of, 7–8
    NLF and, 54
    Vietnam War and, 4–6, 9, 9–11
Kepenevich, Andrew, 51
Kerry, John, 27, 135
Khalilzad, Zalmay, 133
Khmer Rouge, 144–45
King, Martin Luther, 32
Kissinger, Henry, 16, 119, 126–28
    foreign policy and, 157–58
    Vietnam Syndrome and, 140–41,
        142
Korean War, 55, 103, 139
Kosovo, 74
Kristol, Irving, 16
Kristol, William, 17, 158, 160
Krondracke, Morton, 109
Kutner, Robert, 114

Laird, Melvin, 47–48, 50–51, 84, 125
Laos, 4, 46, 127
Lebanon, 147, 148
Le Duan, 10
Le Duc Tho, 129
Le Loi, 77
limited-war theory, 6–9
Lippmann, Walter, 111–112
Logevall, Fred, 6
Lon Nol, 144
Lynch, Jessica, 67

MACV. See Military Assistance Com-
    mand-Vietnam
MAD. See mutually assured destruc-
    tion
Maddox, USS, 22, 23
Madison, James, 14, 29
Mahdi Army, 14, 130, 131
Makiya, Kanan, 72
Mansfield, Mike, 117
Mao Tse-tung, 60
McCain, John, 27, 35, 115–16
McGovern, George, 119
McNamara, Robert S., 6, 8, 10, 22,
    23–24, 114, 117, 122–23, 124
Meany, George, 21
media. See press
Mekong River Development Project,
    19–20, 44, 95–96
Middle East
    democracy in, xii, xiv, 15–16, 17, 31,
        104
    geopolitical future of, ix
    War in Iraq and, ix
Military Assistance Command-Viet-
    nam (MACV), 45, 110
MOBE. See National Mobilization
    Committee to End the War in
    Vietnam
modernization, nation building and,
    95–96
Morse, Wayne, 24
Moscow Summer Olympics (1980),
    143
Moyers, Bill, 19–20
MPLA. See Popular Movement for
    the Liberation of Angola
Mueller, John, 104–5, 145, 167
Murtha, John, 114–15

mutually assured destruction (MAD), 7

My Lai Massacre, 66

Nash, William, 115

national armies
  nation building and, 79–90
  training of, 82–84, 85–86

National Intelligence Estimates, 123

nationalism, pan-Arab, 58

National Liberation Front (NLF), 44, 129
  agenda of, 52
  Iraq insurgency vs., 52, 56–57
  military component of, 53–54
  superpower allies of, xi
  terrorism and, 53
  Vietnamese Communist Party and, 52, 54–55
  Vietnam War and, 44, 52–58

National Mobilization Committee to End the War in Vietnam (MOBE), 135

National Press Club, 107, 146

national security
  cold war and, 7
  democracy and, xiii, 15, 18, 138
  expansionism and, 1–2, 30
  U. S. power and, 3
  Vietnam War and, 117
  War in Iraq and, ix, 27

National Security Memorandum No. 288, 11

The National Security Strategy of the United States of America (NSS) (2002), 14

nation building

Bush, George W. and, xi, 20, 69–70, 75, 79, 201
  costs of, 69
  democracy promotion and, 70, 71, 93–94, 99–102
  economic aspects of, 71, 73
  Future of Iraq Project and, 71–72
  in Iraq, xi, xiv, 20, 69–76, 79–82, 84–87, 89–90, 92–102
  modernization and, 95–96
  nation, defining and, 74–79
  national armies and, 79–90, 82–84
  political aspects of, 73
  sectarian violence and, xi
  social aspects of, xi, 71, 72, 73
  social progress and, xi
  socioeconomic viability and, 91–95
  state and individual and, 96–102
  in Vietnam, xi, 74, 76–79, 91–92, 95–98, 101–2

NATO. See North Atlantic Treaty Organization

Negroponte, John, 73

neoconservatives
  agenda of, xiv
  cold war and, 17
  communism and, 16–17
  democracy promotion and, 137, 160–61, 163, 165–66
  foreign policy agenda of, 157–58
  Iraq Syndrome and, 166
  U. S. power and, 137
  Vietnam Syndrome and, 157–61
  War in Iraq and, xiv
  War on Terror and, 160

New Deal, 18–19

New Iraqi Army (NIA)

military operations and, 86–87
nation building and, 80–82
training of, 85–86
New Look, 6–7
Newsweek, 114, 139
New York Times, 110, 114, 155
New Zealand, 36
Ngo Dinh Diem, 9–10, 24, 43, 52,
53–54, 55, 66
Ngo Dinh Nhu, 9, 10
Nguyen Cao Ky, 78–79, 130
Nguyen van Thieu, 93, 98, 128–30
NIA. *See* New Iraqi Army
Nitze, Paul, 132
Nixon, Richard, 116
"decent interval" and, 126–28
Vietnamization and, 84
Vietnam War, public support for
and, xii, 112, 118–19
Vietnam War and, 47–48
NLF. *See* National Liberation Front
nobility of purpose, xiii, 2, 138
North Atlantic Treaty Organization
(NATO), 6, 121
NSS. *See* *The National Security Strategy
of the United States of America*
(2002)

Office for Reconstruction and
Humanitarian Assistance
(ORHA), 71–72
Oman, 143
Operation Rolling Thunder, 38–39, 44
ORHA. *See* Office for Reconstruction
and Humanitarian Assistance
Osgood, Robert, 7

pacification, 47–50
Pakistan, 143, 144
Palmer, Bruce, 8
pan-Arabism, 58, 59
Paris peace accords (1973), 37, 62
PAVN. *See* People's Army of Vietnam
(PAVN)
Pentagon, 64, 71, 73
People's Army of Vietnam (PAVN)
Vietnam War military operations
and, 42, 44
Vietnam War size and scope and,
36, 37
People's Liberation Armed Forces
(PLAF)
pacification strategy and, 47–49
Vietnam War military operations
and, 42, 44
Vietnam War size and scope and,
36
Perle, Richard, 72
Pew Trust, 165
Philippines, 4, 36
Pillar, Paul, 70–71
PLAF. *See* People's Liberation Armed
Forces
Polk, James K., 29, 30
Popular Movement for the Liberation
of Angola (MPLA), 142
Powell, Colin
credibility, theory of and, 120
First Gulf War and, xiv
foreign policy and, 149–54
Powell Doctrine and, 149–54, 159
War in Iraq and, 12–13, 25–26, 28,
39–40
Power. *See* U. S. power
Power, Samantha, 156

preemption, 2, 31
Present Dangers (Kristol and Kagan), 17
press
  Vietnam War, public support for
    and, 108–13
  War in Iraq and, 109

Rand report, 73–74
REA. *See* Rural Electrification
  Administration
Reagan, Ronald, 116
  foreign policy of, 146–49, 161
Record, Jeffrey, 80
Renan, Ernest, 74–75
Republican Party, Republicans
  domino theory and, 4
  Vietnam War and, 119
Republic of Vietnam Armed Forces
  (RVNAF), 80–81
  military operations and, 87–89
  as national army, 82–84
  Vietnam War size and scope and,
    36
Reuters, 110
Rivers, Mendel, 118
Roosevelt, Franklin D., 14, 18–19
Rostow, Walter, 95, 123–24
Rumsfeld, Donald, 28, 71, 114, 124–25,
  136
Rural Electrification Administration
  (REA), 19
Rusk, Dean, 6, 12, 22–23
Russell, Richard, 117
RVNAF
. *See* Republic of Vietnam Armed
  Forces
Rwanda, xv, 155, 156

Sadr, Muqtada al-, 14, 58, 130
Saudi Arabia, 152
Schell, Jonathan, 5–6
Schelling, Thomas, 7
Schlesinger, James, 141, 151
Schwarzkopf, Norman, 39, 152
SDI. *See* Strategic Defense Initiative
"search and destroy" strategy, 45–46
SEATO. *See* Southeast Asia Treaty
  Organization
The Second Indochina War (Turley), 48
Selective Service Act of 1940, 63–64
Selective Service System, 64
September 11, 14, 15, 159, 160
Sharp, Grant, 23
Sheehan, Cindy, 136
Sheehan, Neil, 110, 111
Shiites
  Iraq insurgency and, 13–14, 58
  nation building and, 81
Shultz, George, 146–48
Singapore, 100
Slocombe, Walter, 86
Somalia, 74, 143
Sorley, Lewis, 49–50
Southeast Asia Treaty Organization
  (SEATO), 6, 121
South Korea, 36
Soviet Union
  nuclear capabilities of, 7–8
  Vietnamese Communists and, xi
  Vietnam War and, xi, 9, 37
Stalin, Joseph, 16
State Department, 39, 71
Strategic Defense Initiative (SDI), 149
Strategic Hamlet Program, 43
Summers, Harry, 141
Sunnis

Iraq insurgency and, 13, 58, 59
nation building and, 81–82
Sun Tzu, 150
Supreme Command (Cohen), 15
Supreme Council for the Islamic Revolution in Iraq (al-Majlis al-A'la lil-Thawara al'Islamiyya fil-'Iraq), 58

Taiwan, 100
TAL. *See* Transitional Administrative Law
Taliban, 58, 131, 158–59
Tennessee Valley Authority (TVA), 19, 95
terrorism
democracy and, 20
Hussein, Saddam and, 15, 28
Iraq and, xii, 2, 26, 28
NLF and, 53
War in Iraq and, 12, 13
See also War on Terror
Tet offensive (1968), 46, 108, 108–9, 132, 141
Thailand, 4, 36, 100
Thieu, Nguyen van. *See* Nguyen van Thieu
Time magazine, 66
Townshend, Charles, 75
Transitional Administrative Law (TAL), 101
Trotsky, Leon, 16
Truman, Harry, 121–22, 132
Turkey, 75–76
Turley, William, 48
Turner, Frederick Jackson, 2
Turner, Nick, 110

TVA. *See* Tennessee Valley Authority
The Twenty-five-Year War (Palmer), 8

UN. *See* United Nations
United Nations Security Council, 27, 28
United Nations (UN), 12, 28–29, 73, 158
human rights and, 155–56
United Press International, 110
U. S. army
in Vietnam War, x, 35–36, 62–66
in War in Iraq, x, 35–36, 62, 66–67
U. S. power
American ideals, exporting and, 19
Bush, George W. and, xiv, 138
Congress and, 3
democracy promotion and, 160–61
foreign policy and, xv
idealism and, 3, 138
Johnson, Lyndon B. and, xiii–xiv, 138
limits of, 4
national security and, 3
neoconservatives and, 137
Vietnam War and, xiii, xiv–xv, 137–40, 156
War in Iraq and, xiii, xiv–xv, 17, 137–40, 156
U. S. Senate Foreign Relations Committee, 105, 135

Valenti, Jack, 21
Vann, John Paul, 110

Vietcong. *See* People's Liberation
  Armed Forces (PLAF)
Vietnam
  democracy in, 101–2
  economic development of, 19–21
  France and, 4–5, 80
  national army in, 82–84
  nation building in, xi, 74, 76–79,
    91–92, 95–98, 101–2
  regime change in, 9–10
  socioeconomic viability and,
    91–92
  See also Vietnam Syndrome; Vietnam
    War
Vietnamese Communist Party
  China and, xi
  nationalism and, 77
  NLF and, 52, 54–55
  Soviet Union and, xi
  superpower allies of, xi
Vietnam Information Group, 107
Vietnamization, 84–85
Vietnam Syndrome, xiv, xv, 126
  Bush, George H. W. and, 152–53
  Carter administration and, 142–46
  Clinton administration and, 155–57
  First Gulf War (1990–1991) and,
    152–54
  foreign policy and, xiv, xv, 140–61
  neoconservatives and, 157–61
  Powell Doctrine and, 149–54
  Reagan administration and,
    146–49
  See also Vietnam; Vietnam War
Vietnam Veterans Against the War
  (VVAW), 135, 136
Vietnam War
  air component of, x, 37–41

American ideals, exporting and,
    18–21
  antiwar protesting and, 134–35
  casualties in, 40–42, 103
  China and, xi, 8–9, 37
  communism and, x, 2, 19
  congressional support for, 21–22,
    24–25, 30, 116–18
  counterinsurgency in, 42–44
  credibility, theory of and, 5–6, 9,
    11, 12, 31, 120–25
  domino theory and, 3–6
  expansionism and, 31
  foreign policy and, 139–40
  funding, 131–33
  goal of, xiii, 8, 138
  Gulf of Tonkin Resolution (1964)
    and, 24–25, 29, 32, 119
  heightened threat perceptions
    and, 1, 30
  idealism and, 1, 5, 18–21, 138, 139
  as insurgency, x, 35
  insurgency in, 52–58
  limited-war theory and, 6–9
  military operations in, x, 42–50
  My Lai Massacre and, 66
  national army in, 87–89
  national security and, 117
  NLF and, 44, 52–58
  nobility of purpose and, 138
  Operation Rolling Thunder and,
    38–39, 44
  original justification for, 3–6
  pacification and, 47–50
  Paris peace accords (1973) and, 37,
    62
  political support for, 1
  press and, 108–13

Vietnam War (*cont.*)
  promoting, 105–7, 107–8
  public support for, xii–xiii, 103–13
  size and scope of, x, 36–42
  Soviet Union and, xi, 9, 37
  Tet offensive (1968) and, 46, 108,
    108–9, 132, 141
  U. S. army in, x, 35–36, 62–66
  U. S. power and, xiii, xiv–xv, 17,
    137–40, 156
  U. S. withdrawal and, 125–30
  Vietnam syndrome and, xiv, xv,
    126
  See also Vietnam Syndrome; Vietnam
    War
Vo Nguyen Giap, 23
VVAW. *See* Vietnam Veterans Against
  the War

War in Iraq
  Abu Ghraib prison scandal and,
    67, 109
  air component of, x, 37–40
  antiwar protesting and, 135–36
  casualties in, 41–42, 103
  congressional support for, xii,
    25–29, 30, 103, 113–16
  costs of, ix, xii
  counterinsurgency in, 50–52
  credibility, theory of and, 124–25
  democracy and, 12, 13, 15–16
  enemy combatants in, 37
  funding, 131, 133–34, 163–64
  goal of, xiii, 138
  as guerrilla war, x, 35
  heightened threat perceptions
    and, 1, 30, 104

  idealism and, xiv, 1, 138
  insurgency and, ix, 13–14, 52, 56–62
  international community and, 28
  Iraq Syndrome and, xiv, xv, 126,
    163–167
  Middle East, democracy in and,
    ix, xii, xiv, 15–16, 17, 31
  military operations in, x, 42
  national security and, ix, 27
  neoconservatives and, xiv
  nobility of purpose and, 138
  original justification for, 3, 12–16
  political war in, 51, 61, 62, 68
  press and, 109
  public support for, xii–xiii, 28,
    103–5, 105–6
  as revolutionary, 12
  sectarian violence and, 90, 126,
    163, 164
  September 11 and, 14
  size and scope of, x, 36, 37, 40
  terrorism and, 12, 13
  U. S. army in, x, 35–36, 62, 66–67
  U. S. foreign policy and, ix, xi
  U. S. power and, xiii, xiv–xv, 17,
    137–40, 156
  U. S. withdrawal and, 125–26,
    130–31
  Vietnam War, lessons of, and, xiv
  War on Terror and, 13, 14
  WMDs and, x, xii, 2, 13, 26, 28
War on Terror
  Bush, George W. and, 160–61
  Congress and, 159–60
  neoconservatives and, 160
  War in Iraq and, 13, 14
  See also terrorism
War Powers Act, 30

War Powers Resolution, 159
Washington Post, 110, 114
Watergate, 119
weapons of mass destruction
    (WMDs)
    Hussein, Saddam and, 2, 13, 26, 28
    War in Iraq and, x, xii, 2, 13, 26, 28
Weinberger, Caspar, 146–47, 149, 150
Weinberger Doctrine, 146–49
Westmoreland, William, 8, 118
    attrition strategy of, 45–47, 51, 141
    RVNAF and, 87–88
    Vietnam War, promoting and, 107

Wilson, Harold, 121
Wilson, Woodrow, xiii, 18, 30, 158
Winning Modern Wars (Clark), 162
Wolfowotz, Paul, 16, 17, 66–67, 158
World War I, 75
World War II, 36, 38, 133

Zakaria, Fareed, 100
Zarqawi, Abu Musab al-, 13, 58
Zhou En-lai, 126–27
Zilmer, Richard, 94
Zinni, Anthony, 115

PublicAffairs is a publishing house founded in 1997. It is a tribute to the standards, values, and flair of three persons who have served as mentors to countless reporters, writers, editors, and book people of all kinds, including me.

I.F. STONE, proprietor of *I. F. Stone's Weekly*, combined a commitment to the First Amendment with entrepreneurial zeal and reporting skill and became one of the great independent journalists in American history. At the age of eighty, Izzy published *The Trial of Socrates*, which was a national bestseller. He wrote the book after he taught himself ancient Greek.

BENJAMIN C. BRADLEE was for nearly thirty years the charismatic editorial leader of *The Washington Post*. It was Ben who gave the *Post* the range and courage to pursue such historic issues as Watergate. He supported his reporters with a tenacity that made them fearless and it is no accident that so many became authors of influential, best-selling books.

ROBERT L. BERNSTEIN, the chief executive of Random House for more than a quarter century, guided one of the nation's premier publishing houses. Bob was personally responsible for many books of political dissent and argument that challenged tyranny around the globe. He is also the founder and longtime chair of Human Rights Watch, one of the most respected human rights organizations in the world.

*

For fifty years, the banner of Public Affairs Press was carried by its owner Morris B. Schnapper, who published Gandhi, Nasser, Toynbee, Truman, and about 1,500 other authors. In 1983, Schnapper was described by *The Washington Post* as "a redoubtable gadfly." His legacy will endure in the books to come.

Peter Osnos, *Founder and Editor-at-Large*